"THE COGNOSCENTI"

The ruling political class who thinks it knows
better than everyone else

RONALD JOSEPH HIGBY JR

Contents

Preface   **v**

Introduction   **ix**

Part I: The Federal Constitution, Statism and the Cognoscenti   **1**

     1. The "Apple of Gold," the "Frame of Silver" and Statism   3

     2. The progressive movement and eroding the
federal constitution   23

     3. The cognoscenti: a new aristocracy and academic
indoctrination   55

     4. Tipping into majority tyranny and soft despotism   75

Part II: Reversing the statist erosion of the federal Constitution   **91**

     5. Become a knowledgeable citizen   93

     6. Reform government spending and
reduce federal deficits   101

     7. Reform the federal tax code and
increase revenues   111

     8. Reclaim control over public education   115

     9. Fight to avoid an inevitable serfdom   127

Appendix: Sources available to become a more knowledgeable
citizen   135

Notes   139

Bibliography   151

PREFACE

When surveying the government's actions over the last seven decades, one sees an increasing pattern of centralized government, an increasing number of government workers, an increasing flood of regulations, and an increasing intrusiveness into the everyday lives of Americans. Most Americans seem oblivious to the underlying premise of progressivism/statism dating from the early twentieth century, when Woodrow Wilson, Franklin Roosevelt, and Lyndon Johnson persuaded the Congress to put in place social programs not anticipated in the Constitution. By so doing, the purpose of government was altered fundamentally from protecting individuals' rights to life, liberty, and the pursuit of happiness to providing benefits and redistributing income in the name of social justice.

Social planners institute these programs of providing benefits—social security, Medicare, welfare, unemployment insurance, and so forth—and a progressive tax collection that excludes nearly half the population. They believe they know better than we do and can make better decisions. Many of them are university and college faculty members, and they manifest intellectual arrogance and presumptuousness. They are true *cognoscenti*—a term used primarily among the aesthetic elements of American society meaning "a person with superior, usually specialized knowledge or highly refined taste; a connoisseur."[1] I've borrowed and adapted this term to refer to politicians and bureaucrats who maintain that government should be more centralized; who adopt higher expenditures of taxpayer dollars; who borrow forty cents of every dollar spent to keep the present status quo; and who adopt thousands of pages of regulations intruding on the business and private lives of citizens. They embrace the progressive/statist agenda, or what some call modern liberalism (also called the left, left wing, leftist, and radical leftist). If using the term the Cognoscenti catches on, perhaps the media—print, television, and electronic—and others involved with political commentary all could consistently use this one term so everyone would know immediately who was being described and what platform they advocate.

Nineteenth-century progressivism has an underlying premise of statism, that is, making the State a priority over the individual. Progressives believe in a "living Constitution." They do not believe the words of the Constitution should be understood as they were in the eighteenth century. Instead the Constitution should be adapted to the conditions that exist today.

Most Americans understand the game of baseball and the rules that make the game enjoyable. The rules tell an umpire where the strike zone is: between a batter's elbows and knees. Umpires may differ in just how precisely they see that area, but they do not have the authority to disregard it. Well, the Constitution provides the rules of the game for all Americans. Saying that we have a "living Constitution" is like an umpire deciding the strike zone will be from the tip of the batter's nose to his toes for today's game in order to adapt to current conditions. This is the difference between an originalist interpretation (sticking to what the Constitution says) and a "living Constitution" interpretation (adapting to conditions, such as allowing a right to privacy that is not explicitly granted in the Constitution).

This book has been a work in progress for the past ten years, ever since I retired from my position as a deputy city manager after twenty-nine years of local government service, primarily in the field of human resources. It started with the intention of passing on some memoirs to my grandchildren. My concern was the cultural divide in America between two seemingly irreconcilable views of the world. As I progressed, I was unsure of just how I was going to compile a book that would appeal to a publisher. Fortunately, I was guided into self-publishing, and I am very pleased that I went through Amazon to locate a self-publishing resource: CreateSpace. I want to thank Katie Davis, publishing consultant, the editorial staff, and Molly, Adam, Emily and all the rest of the project team at CreateSpace, as well as my family and friends who read drafts at different stages and gave me valuable and pungent criticism.

I want to thank my wife, friend, and confidante Mary Jane (nee Capp). We went to Italy more than twenty years ago and learned about Michelangelo, who said when he sculpted a statue that it just emerged from the marble. Mary Jane, I am most grateful to you for hanging in there with me as this book emerged from my "marble" of reading and trial and error.

Finally, I want to thank and dedicate this book to our children and grandchildren starting with Brian and Kelly Nelson, and their children Brian, James, Georgia Franklin, and Camryn Nelson; Clarise and Mort O'Connor and their daughter, Cassidy; David and Janelle Nelson, and their son, August; Erin and Joe Page, and their children, Kanon and Kortlyn; and Brett and Traci Higby, and their children Owen and London. It is they and their progeny that are on the road to an inevitable serfdom.

In the 1940s, Nobel economist Friedrich von Hayek wrote *The Road to Serfdom*, which warned about the consequences of social planning. He reminded readers of life during feudal times, when the common people were known as serfs. They were not slaves; however, they were in bondage to the lord of the manor. In like manner, Hayek visualized a similar result for modern-day citizens falling into a new variation of bondage. In honor of his knowledgeable warning, I conclude this book with a similar warning that America is on the road to an inevitable serfdom and must act now to return to the principles of constitutional conservatism that is the legacy from our Founding Fathers.

INTRODUCTION

My main point in writing this book is to alert Americans to the dangers of an irrevocable loss of liberty that is the consequence of the over-spending, over-borrowing, and over regulation by the ruling class. The main problem in America today is the government.

I am concerned about the politicians' promises that have translated into programs employing millions of government workers. They spend $7.6 trillion each year, collect $6.2 trillion in taxes and other revenues, and borrow $4 billion each day or $1.46 trillion per year just to maintain the status quo.

I am also concerned that the national debt has increased from $10 trillion to $15 trillion in just the last three years and is now approximately equal to the entire annual gross domestic product.

I do not believe Americans understand Progressivism or its underlying premise of statism, which originated with nineteenth-century German philosophers and shared an intellectual foundation with both Italian and Spanish fascism and German Nazism. *Statism* (state-ism) refers to glorification of the state or nation over and above individual's rights to life, liberty, and the pursuit of happiness. Statism concentrates political and economic power in the central government to solve societal problems.

As explained in the preface, in order to help readers focus on the source of the problem, I use the term *Cognoscenti* to describe the elected politicians and un-elected bureaucrats that constitute the ruling class in America today. Of course not everyone elected to office or appointed as a government bureaucrat necessarily shares the same progressive/statist worldview. When they behave the same way—over-spending, over-borrowing and over-regulating—then they are opportunists taking advantage of present-day power and control realities.

I am concerned that many intellectuals and scholars who pursue the progressive/statist agenda have teaching positions in our colleges, universities, and public high schools through which they can indoctrinate the impressionable youth to see the world from their point of view. I am concerned that part of this indoctrination pattern is to avoid teaching about individual rights, equality before the law, and traditional values. Instead they choose to emphasize that equality means equality of outcomes and redistribution of wealth in the name of social justice.

If this trend continues, ultimately we will lose our liberty and sink into a soft despotism. In a future America, the Democratic Party could become the nucleus of a Majority Party. This brings to mind George Orwell's *Nineteen Eighty-Four*, in which the Outer Party members did most of the work, and the Inner Party ruled everything and everyone. Membership in the party determined who would or would not succeed in politics and business. Orwell's tyrannical Thought Police reminds one of the abundance of rules and regulations and the hordes of enforcement officers now employed by the federal government.

For eight decades Americans have failed to pay attention to the erosion of the constitutional limits on the federal government. It's reaching the point where we've virtually returned to a condition of unlimited government.

This book is divided into two parts. Part I examines how American government came into being. For Abraham Lincoln, the Declaration of Independence was an "apple of gold," the federal Constitution was the "frame of silver" giving it form, and the Civil War established clearly that all men are born equal under the law. Persuaded by German professors that statism was superior to republican democracy, the intellectual godfathers of the American progressive movement sought to find ways around the Constitution to achieve an agenda based upon redistribution of wealth and social justice. From 1913 to the present day, the Cognoscenti succeeded in concentrating political and economic power in the central government. Because of the human tendency to want to work and live with those most like oneself, the faculty and administrators who hire and promote within our schools tend to choose those who are like-minded and to reject those who hold differing viewpoints, especially constitutional conservatives. As a result, students are increasingly exposed to only one point of view when it comes to the purpose of government and what it means to be a citizen. America is now at the tipping point of slipping into a majority tyranny and soft despotism.

In Part II there are five suggestions for reversing this progressive/statist erosion of the federal Constitution. First, everyone needs to know the enemy, to be knowledgeable, and to defend the Second and Tenth amendments. Second, everyone must support efforts to reform and reduce federal deficits, excessive government spending, and the national debt. Third, everyone must support reform of the federal tax code and have a higher percentage of Americans paying a share of the income tax. Fourth, everyone must support efforts to reclaim control over public education. Finally, everyone needs to participate in the fight against an inevitable serfdom. At this time the Tea Party movement stands out as the best option to identify replacements for present members of the Cognoscenti. As a nation, we enjoy liberty and benefits passed on by those who have gone before us. Now, we too have an opportunity to honor the signers of the Declaration of Independence, who each pledged "their life, fortune, and sacred honor." In like manner, we now must similarly pledge our "life, fortune and sacred honor" to act responsibly on the imperative of electing to Congress representatives who will implement spending, taxation, and regulatory reforms that will correct the terrible erosion of our constitutional liberties.

PART I:

THE FEDERAL CONSTITUTION, STATISM AND THE COGNOSCENTI

Constitutional conservatism had its roots in the 182 years of local and colonial government experience that differs significantly from the history of most of the other modern democratic nations. The Declaration of Independence ("apple of gold") and the federal Constitution ('frame of silver") are the foundation. The *Federalist Papers* explained the advantages of the Federal Constitution. Before *Manifest Destiny* could be realized, a terrible civil war had to resolve the issue of slavery. The "Gilded Age" ushered in a period of opportunity for many and fabulous wealth for a few. German philosophers influenced American scholars with an idea of statism and a progressive agenda that was intended to undermine the work of the Founding Fathers.

Teddy Roosevelt, a hero of the Spanish American War became the first unofficial progressive president in 1901. Then, in a three-way 1912 election, Woodrow Wilson was the first authentic progressive president. Thereafter, a concerted progressive/statist erosion of the federal Constitution commenced from 1913 through 2009. Today, there is an Iron Triangle – comprised of politicians, bureaucrats and beneficiaries of government programs.

A new aristocracy - the Cognoscenti - perpetuates itself and is highly compensated. Many Cognoscenti come from academia that embrace the progressive/statist agenda. In the classrooms, indoctrination erodes understanding of natural rights and limited government. Many graduates become teachers, professors, journalists, lawyers and judges perpetuating the progressive/statist agenda.

Tyranny prevailed under some variation of the "divine right of kings" for nearly 5,000 years. In addition, there was the reality that pure democracy can lead to either oligarchy or majority tyranny. After establishing a representative democracy, Tocqueville was among the first to utter warnings about the dangers of soft despotism. Now, the Democratic Party has the potential of becoming the nucleus of a majority tyranny. Also, President Obama, as a demagogue, has the potential to transform America into a perpetual soft despotism.

1. The "Apple of Gold," the "Frame of Silver" and Statism

Constitutional conservatism had its roots in the 168 years of local and colonial government experience that differs significantly from the history of most of the other modern democratic nations. The Declaration of Independence ("apple of gold") and the federal Constitution ("frame of silver") are the foundation. The *Federalist Papers* explained the advantages of the Federal Constitution. Before Manifest Destiny could be realized, a terrible civil war had to resolve the issue of slavery. The "Gilded Age" ushered in a period of opportunity for many and fabulous wealth for a few. German philosophers influenced American scholars with an idea of statism and a progressive agenda that was intended to undermine the work of the Founding Fathers.

Colonial America and the ruling class

Prior to the adoption of the Federal Constitution, the English colonists enjoyed up to 182 years experience of citizen participation in both local and colonial government. The existence of semi-independent colonies and all this experience with governance provided a foundation for later nationhood that has not been enjoyed anywhere else in the world since that time. The crown appointed the governors and the governor's council (which approximated the House of Lords in parliament). The colonists elected their representatives in the Assembly (which approximated the House of Commons). The assembly had complete control over the budget and the levying of taxes. The governor appointed judges to the local courts. This three-branch form of government set the pattern for national, state, and local governments in the future.

Those born in the colonies identified themselves as citizens of the colony in which they were born and lived, that is, Virginian, Pennsylvanian, New Yorker, and so forth. There was no concept of being an "American." Unlike their forebears who had, for thousands of years, lived under some form of tyranny (unlimited government predicated upon centralized rule), the new settlers governed themselves by establishing limited government. Citizens knew their representatives, paid attention to their actions, and held them accountable. For the most part, small towns and settlements corresponded to the kinship groups, such as band and tribe, of primitive times. Another important aspect of the colonial experience was the absence of a formal privileged aristocracy. While younger sons of English aristocracy established many of the plantations of the southern colonies, there are very few examples in the English colonies of a privileged, nonworking class as compared to the *caballeros* in the Spanish and Portuguese colonies in what today is known as Latin America.

The colonies had an economic ruling class, of sorts. In New England and the middle colonies, the merchants, bankers, traders, and ship owners were wealthier and were, in effect, an economic ruling class. In the southern colonies, the plantation owners were a ruling class, for they exercised both economic and political influence. This happened because they were usually the only ones selected for the governor's council (the upper house of the legislature) and they also dominated membership in the lower house of the legislature.

Generally, the other colonists accepted these conditions. Most of them had endured a class system in their country of origin that had a royal government supported by an aristocracy. When arriving in the colonies, there was never a formal installation of an aristocracy. Instead, land ownership, or financial affluence, became the basis of setting apart an informal ruling class.

The "Apple of Gold"—the Declaration of Independence

Abraham Lincoln used the metaphor "apple of gold" to refer to the Declaration of Independence and "frame of silver" to refer to the US Constitution in an unpublished letter, according to Kevin Porteus. This insight was presented in a lecture that was part of a Hillsdale College video presentation of *Constitution 101*.[1] Lincoln wanted to emphasize the foundational importance of the Declaration, which asserts that all men are born equal with natural rights to life, liberty, and the pursuit of happiness. Those rights are as precious as an "apple of gold." The primary purpose of government is to protect those natural rights, and the Constitution was composed to give effect to that purpose. The Constitution then becomes a "frame of silver" around the "apple of gold."

John Locke (1632-1704) published his *Second Treatise of Government* after the English Parliament passed a Bill of Rights in 1689. Based on his experiences, and using reason to make assumptions about the nature of government and man's place in it, Locke reached important conclusions that had bearing on the subsequent American Revolution. He argued for an individual natural right to unlimited property and the necessity of a limited constitutional state to protect that right. His chapter on property states "it fixed property rights firmly in the center of all subsequent liberal theory; and it is essential to an understanding of Locke's chain of argument from the state of nature to the limited and conditional nature of governments' powers."[2]

Locke goes on to make the argument that, once established, any part of government is revocable. The authority of any government is conditional on its performing the functions for which it was entrusted with power. When a government behaves in an unjust manner, it is the government, not those subjects who resist it, that is guilty of rebellion. Locke thus asserts a right of revolution.[3]

These ideas of Locke were familiar to the representatives who convened the Second Continental Congress in Philadelphia on May 10, 1775, and proceeded to act as the de facto national government. Over the course of the next twelve months, the thirteen separate colonial governments debated and discussed the problem of reconciliation or independence. In June 1776 a committee was appointed to draft a declaration of independence; it included Thomas Jefferson, John Adams, Benjamin Franklin, Roger Livingston, and Roger Sherman, each of whom is now considered a Founding Father of the American republic. Jefferson was asked to write a first draft.

He followed Locke's general principles contained in a twenty-seven-paragraph bill of particulars, published in 1689, that listed how the British government had taken away the rights of the colonists.

In the opening paragraphs, Jefferson invoked natural law in support of the claim that the King had violated the colonists' rights. Like Locke, Jefferson argued that all men are created equal, they enjoy certain natural rights, they create governments to defend these rights, governmental authority rests on the consent of the governed, and that consent can be withdrawn if the government becomes destructive of those rights. Joseph Melusky makes this observation:

> Locke's argument asserts that all men are created equal before the law; that unalienable rights—life, liberty and pursuit of happiness—come from their Creator, not from government. A just government exists to secure these rights and resides on the consent of the governed, not the divine right of kings. When government becomes unjust, it is the right of the people to alter or abolish that government and fashion a government that will exist to protect their safety and happiness, without excessive government taxation, regulation and interference.[4]

The Congress approved Jefferson's draft of the Declaration of Independence. Lincoln's "house divided against itself cannot stand" applies to present time America. Citizens must be willing to pledge "their lives, fortunes, and sacred honor." On July 4, 1776, the fifty-six men who signed the document did so with full knowledge that they were risking everything to establish independence from Great Britain. They each solemnly pledged "and for the support of this Declaration, with a firm Reliance on the Protection of divine Providence, we mutually pledge to each other our Lives, our Fortunes, and our sacred Honor." Rush Limbaugh briefly summarizes what happened to some of the delegates:

> There are many harrowing tales about what happened to the delegates afterward. Francis Lewis, New York delegate, saw his home plundered and his estates in what is now

Harlem completely destroyed by British soldiers. William Floyd, another New York delegate, was able to escape with his family to Connecticut, where they lived as refugees without income for seven years. When they came home they found a devastated ruin. Philips Livingstone had all his great holdings in New York confiscated and his family driven out of their home. John Hart of Trenton, New Jersey, risked his life to return home to see his dying wife. Hessian soldiers chased him into the woods. His 13 children were taken away and he never saw them again. … Edward Rutledge, Arthur Middleton, and Thomas Heyward, Jr. were taken by the British in the siege of Charleston and sent as prisoners of war to St. Augustine. They returned after the war to find their large landholdings and estates completely devastated. … Thomas Nelson became Governor of Virginia and was serving at Yorktown where Cornwallis was besieged. When artillery was making a shambles of the town his estate remained untouched out of respect to him. Nelson cried, "Give me the cannon!" and he fired on his magnificent home himself. Nelson mortgaged his estate to raise millions for the war effort. Afterwards, when the loans came due, Congress refused to honor them. He died, impoverished, a few years later at the age of 50. [5]

The Treaty of Paris (1783) ended the American Revolutionary War, and each colony became an independent sovereign state organized into a confederation of states. For thousands of years of recorded history, confederations of independent states had most often failed because of the difficulty in finding common ground on which to unify for military assistance, to exercise control over foreign affairs, to raise taxes, and to support a common currency. All confederations suffered from the same weakness: requiring approval from each of the independent entities before constructive action could be taken. In today's European Union, we see an example of an economic union that suffers from the same handicaps as a political confederation. Under the Articles of

Confederation, the thirteen new sovereign states were unable to raise taxes for the central government and were unable to resolve how the war debts should be paid. Because of a ruinous financial depression after the war, a mutiny of farmers in Massachusetts (Shay's Rebellion in the summer 1786) highlighted the weakness of the confederation.

The "Frame of Silver"—the US Constitution

Government exists to protect the natural rights of the individual. The states and the people, acting through the Founding Founders, composed the federal Constitution that established the federal government with enumerated and limited powers.

Delegates replaced the confederation with a federation based on a constitution of enumerated limited powers on September 17, 1787. On May 25 delegates from nine states gathered at Independence Hall in Philadelphia to draft a plan to overcome the perceived weaknesses of the Articles of Confederation. The delegates disagreed on many things, foremost how to form a national legislature. Roger Sherman proposed the Great Compromise or Connecticut Compromise. In this plan the people would be represented proportionally in the House of Representatives (the lower house). The states would be guaranteed equality with two senators each in the Senate (the upper house). When the delegates agreed to this compromise, crafting the balance of constitutional provisions was relatively easy. They also agreed Congress should have the power to lay only direct taxes and the states would retain determination of voting qualifications (suffrage requirements).

The Federalist Papers Explained the Advantages of Constitution

Alexander Hamilton, James Madison, and John Jay wrote a series of pamphlets arguing for the adoption of the new constitution that was published as the *Federalist Papers*. They signed the pamphlets with the name Publius. Alexander Hamilton began by stating that America was at a crossroads. Glenn Beck is the co-author of *Common Sense*, which takes the Federalist Papers and translates them into modern English. In this section, many quotations are taken from this source:

> The People of this country have been put in the position of deciding a very important question: Are societies capable of freely choosing to establish good government for themselves, or will such thing forever be determined by accident and force. ... If we are to falter now, it would be, in my opinion, to the detriment of all mankind.[6]

"John Jay wrote in Federalist 2, including this paragraph, which shows that Jay believed the concepts of 'one nation' and 'under God' were linked together. 'This country and this people seem to have been made for each other, and it appears as if it was the design of Providence, that an inheritance so proper and convenient for a band of brethren, united to each other by the strongest ties, should never be split into a number of unsocial, jealous, and alien sovereignties. ... Splitting apart would not only be foolish, Jay argued, but it would also be against God's will."[7] Beck summarizes why the Constitution is so important: "Freedom is not the natural state of man. Without a shield in place to protect individual rights and the force to hold that shield strong, freedom becomes fleeting. Tyranny, the natural state of government, inevitably returns. In America, that shield is our Constitution, and the force that allows us to hold it strong is God. The government is not a protector of anything—it is simply an agent of our collective will."[8]

In Federalist 37, James Madison wanted to make one other point extremely clear. There was a big difference between the powers given to the government in the name of national defense and those given in the name of, say, collecting taxes. In Federalist 42, Madison explained why the federal government needed to have the power to regulate commerce with foreign countries and between states and the power of international diplomacy. He argued that chaos would inevitably result if each state were to be in charge of these.[9] In perhaps his most important contribution, Madison rested his case by explaining why government is both necessary and must be limited.

In order to lay a due foundation for that separate and distinct exercise of the different powers of government, which to a certain extent is admitted on all hands to be essential to the preservation of liberty, it is evident that each department should have a will of its own; and consequently should be so constituted that the members of each should has as little agency as possible in the appointment of the members of the other. ... In the constitution of the judiciary department in particular, it might be inexpedient to insist rigorously on the principle: first, because peculiar qualifications being essential in the members, the primary consideration ought to be to select that mode of choice which best secures these qualifications; secondly, because the permanent tenure by which the appointments are held in that department, must soon destroy all sense of dependence on the authority conferring them. But the great security against a gradual concentration of the several powers in the same department, consists in giving to those who administer each department the necessary constitutional means and personal motives to resist encroachments of the others.[10]

Beck stresses why the states are important to help define why the federal government is limited in its powers:

America is a republic and the distinction isn't minor. A *representative democracy*, which more accurately describes our model of government, means that we cede decision-making to our elected officials but maintain ultimate authority through the right to vote. ... Throughout the *Federalist Papers*, readers are reminded that the Constitution would establish a republican government, not a democracy. ... Just as the terms "democracy" and "republic" are often used interchangeably, we often use the terms "national" and "federal" synonymously, but they have very different meanings. "National" refers to a union of all the people of a nation, along with the government duties and policies that promote the common welfare of all people. "Federal," on the other hand, refers to the structure of government that pertains to the union of individual states that combine into a federation. The authors of the *Federalist Papers* continually stressed that states are essential parts of the Constitution and not merely tangential offshoots of the federal government, as they are often treated today. There are some powers that the states retain that the federal government can do nothing to change or affect. The founders believed that the secret was to create a centralized power to maintain unity and order and to deal only with problems that would affect the entire nation. They would leave the rest up to local governments.[11]

Beck then explains why the Electoral College is so significant:

The Founders designed the Electoral College to elect a president to act as a sort of "emotional backstop" that would prevent voters from making ill-informed decisions based purely on a "sudden breeze of passion"... The other big aim of the Electoral College was to find a president who was not so beholden to special interests, or even to his own supporters, that he could not make the right decisions for the country: a president who "would rely on everyone except the People for continuing in his office," as Hamilton put it in Federalist 68.[12]

Next, Beck takes up the topic of when it was necessary to have a strong federal government. "Nevertheless, in times of emergency, there should be no limits on the Federal government having the authority to do whatever is necessary. The states and people gave the central government its power in the first place. … Emergencies could occur, Hamilton explained in Federalist 28, or insurrections might arise that could pose a danger to the republic as a whole. If that were the case then the federal government would have "no remedy but force."

Yes, force. That, of course, is an extraordinarily dangerous power to give to a government. A government's use of force against its own citizens is often the hallmark of tyrannical regimes. So, of course, Hamilton explained, that power needed to be balanced—and he further explained that the Constitution offered two specific ways to do that. First, the system was set up so that the states would always have the opportunity to stand up to the federal government—and vice versa. The second way to balance the power given to the federal government was the cornerstone principle of the entire constitution: power to the people. Hamilton wrote: "There is then no resource left but in the exertion of that original right of self-defense which is paramount to all positive forms of government.... After all, self-defense in the face of an aggressor is a basic right."[13]

Beck continues of the topic of limited government. "Publius hoped to create a central government that could contribute to the people's happiness. However, this could not be achieved by a 'one-size-fits-all' approach to local issues. The Founders understood that local control of local matters makes for far more responsive and agile government—and far happier people. This should strike us as common sense (but how can one explain) why the power of state governments has been shrinking while the power, size, and reach of the federal government has been expanding? … Perhaps Hamilton simply could not imagine that a majority of voters would one day be conned by an increasingly sophisticated and duplicitous government made up of representatives who, by and large, put party and power above principles. Publius didn't foresee—and could not have foreseen— a day in which a debt-laden, money-printing federal government would literally bribe states into agreeing with policies, e.g. highway funds, stimulus grants, or 'Race to the Top' money."[14]

Beck continues with his argument. "Tyranny, of course, was on everyone's mind given what they'd all just been through. Preventing it, therefore, was a top priority. … Instead of laws being contemplated according to their constitutionality, the thinking instead seems to be that Congress should pass whatever laws they like and worry about the courts later. The basis for this view is almost always the so-called 'necessary and proper clause' because people try to use it to justify all sorts of goodies not called for in the Constitution. Some have used these forty-five words to argue that the federal government can make any law it pleases. But Hamilton wrote an argument against that in Federalist 33. (He argued that the) only reason it was being included was to make it perfectly clear that the federal government had the power to make the laws it need to enforce the powers it was being given."[15]

On September 17, 1787, the Constitution was completed with the proviso that only nine states were needed to ratify it. The Congress of the Confederation (the Articles Congress) certified that the new Constitution had been ratified by eleven of the thirteen states on September 13, 1788. On April 30, 1789, George Washington was sworn in as the first president of the United States. The Bill of Rights was adopted in 1791. After the Constitution was ratified in 1789, the resulting Constitution has remained basically unchanged for 223 years, one of the longest ever sustained governmental documents in all the history of Western Civilization. The work of the Founding Fathers was completed. They based their republic on two revolutionary principles—*that all men are created equal* and *that power ultimately derives from the will of the people.*[16]

Lincoln Focused on the "Apple of Gold"

Because of the importance of Jefferson's purchase of the Louisiana Territory, this period of American history (1789-1912) will be lumped together as the period of fulfilling America's *Manifest Destiny*. In 1793 Eli Whitney invented the cotton gin, which had a profound impact, for it once again made slavery profitable. On November 16, 1793, Congress passed the Fugitive Slave Act, which contributed to the later *Dred Scott* Supreme Court decision that was ultimately resolved by the American Civil War.

Caught up in the expenses of war in Europe, Emperor Napoleon sold to President Thomas Jefferson and the United States for $15 million the whole of the Louisiana Territory, an area of approximately 800,000 square miles. This almost doubled the size of the United States and ushered in a period of *Manifest Destiny*. Britain searched American ships and impressed the sailors into the British navy, which prompted a second war with Britain (1812-1814). The war proceeded badly for the US, except for victories at sea by the *USS Constitution* ("Old Ironsides") and Andrew Jackson's victory over the British at New Orleans.

The 1820 Missouri Compromise admitted Missouri as a slave state and Maine as a free state and prohibited slavery in the remainder of the Louisiana Purchase north of the southern boundary of Missouri. Thus Congress legislated against the property rights of those in states that maintained slaves as property. Under the principle of equal protection under the law, this was perceived by plantation owners in the South as unfair in much the same way British taxation without representation was in 1765.

Can the states decide to separate themselves from the Union? Can they secede? More and more southerners decided that this would be the only way to resolve the underlying question with regard to slavery. The Compromise of 1850 admitted California as a free state. In 1852 publication of *Uncle Tom's Cabin* stimulated and provoked abolitionists even more to use the Underground Railroad to free slaves. In 1854 the Republican Party was formed from remnants of the Whig Party and was strongly opposed to slavery and determined to oppose the Kansas-Nebraska Bill. Abraham Lincoln gave a speech in Peoria, Illinois, on October 16, 1854:

> I hate it because of the monstrous injustice of slavery itself. I hate it because it deprives our republican example of its just influence in the world (causing) real friends of freedom to doubt our sincerity, and especially because it forces so many really good men amongst ourselves into an open war with the very fundamental principles of civil liberty—criticizing the Declaration of Independence,

and insisting that there is no right principle of action but *self-interest.*[17]

The *Dred Scott* Supreme Court decision, handed down on March 6, 1857, ruled that slaves were property and had to be returned to their owners under state law. Abraham Lincoln, in a four-person race, was elected sixteenth president in 1860. In 1861 the citizens in the eleven slave-holding states exercised what they believed to be their rights under the Declaration of Independence and the Constitution: they voted to secede from the Union and to form the Confederate States of America.

The American Civil War started when the South Carolina militia captured Fort Sumter in Charleston Harbor on April 12-13, 1861. During the first two years of the war, the North lost most of the battles fought against Confederate defensive positions. The tide turned in 1863 with Union victories at Gettysburg and Vicksburg. General Grant and the Union army forced Gen. Robert E. Lee to surrender at Appomattox on April 9, 1865. By the end of the war, both sides had suffered more than 600,000 casualties—two percent of the nation's total population of thirty million. (With today's population of more than three hundred million, it would be the equivalent of six million casualties.)

President Lincoln's assassination by John Wilkes Booth on April 14, 1865, shocked the nation and made the Reconstruction period longer and harsher than it might have been otherwise. The right of a state to secede from the Union was resolved finally. Once a state became part of the federal Union, it gave up the right of secession. The Presidential Reconstruction Plan of 1867 allowed a coalition of freedmen, scalawags (local whites), and carpetbaggers (recent arrivals) to take control of Southern state governments. Many blacks were elected to political office. However, radical Republicans imposed restrictions that would prevent most ex-rebels from voting or holding office.

With regard to the "apple of gold," let us revisit the original question. People of African descent held as slaves – were they persons or chattel? President Lincoln believed the Declaration of Independence provided that all persons in the United States, regardless of race or economic status, had equal rights to life, liberty, and the pursuit of happiness. This could only mean that they were entitled to equal protection under the Constitution and under the law. Using his powers as commander in chief, he issued the Emancipation Proclamation, in 1862, an executive order freeing the slaves in states that were in rebellion. The final abolition of slavery was achieved by the Thirteenth Amendment, ratified in December 1865. The states ratified the Fourteenth Amendment on July 9, 1868, giving enormous new powers to the federal courts to deal with justice at the state level. The Fifteenth Amendment was ratified in 1870, giving freedmen—but not women—the right to vote in elections.

The Gilded Age

From 1870 until 1912, *Manifest Destiny* helped fill the continent from the Atlantic to the Pacific oceans, and a total of forty-eight states were recognized. During the nineteenth century, immigrants swarmed to America from all over Europe, contributing to a vast increase in farming and manufacturing. In the large urban centers—New York, Boston, Chicago—immigrants tended to cluster together, reemphasizing the importance of tribalism. Many of them came from societies where tyranny was normal and there was no concept of equality or tradition of individual rights. All of this impacted how they and their American-born descendants participated in the political system and how they developed voting patterns.

Because of the enormous wealth of a few men, the era was called the Gilded Age, a term coined by Mark Twain and Charles Dudley Warner in 1873. Note the ironic difference between a *gilded* age and a *golden* age. The powerful industrialists and financiers of the era—Andrew Carnegie, John D. Rockefeller, Jay Gould, and J. P. Morgan—became the nucleus of a class of the super-rich known collectively by their enemies as robber barons. This newly created economic ruling class contributed generously to the construction of hospitals, museums, colleges, opera houses, libraries, and orchestras, then helped the city of Chicago host the World's Columbian Exposition of 1893.

In the West, the Homestead Act of 1862 authorized the federal government to issue 160-acre parcels of land virtually free. New settlers purchased land at very low interest from the new railroads that were trying to create markets. The number of people living on farms grew from about ten million in 1860 to thirty-one million in 1905. Nineteenth-century American farmers experienced recurring cycles of hardship because mechanical improvements greatly increased the yield per unit area. The farther west the settlers went, they increased the amount of land under cultivation and the more dependent they became on the monopolistic railroads to move their goods to market.

By the late nineteenth century, the United States had become a leading industrial power, ushering in a period of rapid economic growth and prosperity. The steady stream of immigrants into the country meant cheap and available labor, especially in the mining and manufacturing sectors. Railroads opened up the West, creating farms, towns, and markets where none had existed. New technologies in iron and steel manufacturing and new communication tools—the telegraph and telephone—allowed corporate managers to coordinate across great distances. In the midst of this prosperity, more and more American students traveled to Europe to study and to obtain graduate degrees. At the time, no one realized how that would contribute to a new worldview emerging to challenge the basic premises established by the Founding Fathers.

German Philosophers and American Statism

During the nineteenth century, German philosophers argued for statism and influenced American scholars who came to Europe to study. Statism emerged as a unifying idea in the nineteenth century thanks to several German philosophers. The Free Online Dictionary provides this definition of statism:

> *Statism.* The practice or doctrine of exalting the nation as an organic body; governing by a Supreme Leader, and unifying through the use of force and discipline. Statism is the

theory or practice of concentrating economic and political power in the state, resulting in a weak position for the individual with respect to the government.

Prior to the adoption of the American federal Constitution, the colonists had upwards of 182 years of experience in self-government and had a clear idea of what it meant to be a citizen. In contrast many of the populations in Europe were still living under some form of feudalism, as they had for centuries. Most common people considered themselves subjects who looked to a single ruler as the source of government.

Georg Wilhelm Friedrich Hegel (1770-1831) and other intellectuals explored the problem of the individual, society, and the state. They concluded that individual self-realization was possible only within society, since individual existence had significance only in society. Self-realization, in effect, meant obedience to authority because the individual will, the true rational will, was part of and expressed in the will of the state. Society was seen as organic, not mechanistic, as having grown over a process of time rather than having resulted from one creative effort, as an inseparable whole rather than a total sum of finite individual entities. In the view of German philosophers, the State was something tangible, something of substance, a place that could give significance to individual existence. The state had a will, a consciousness, and a moral end of its own on a higher level than that of any individual. Moral laws did not limit the State internally or externally, since it was itself the source of such laws.

Hegel suggested everyone could fall into one of three classes: the substantial (agricultural and related manual labor workers); the business (craftsmen, manufacturers, trade, and finance); and the universal (civil servants). Thus Hegel lays a foundation for modern-day Cognoscenti, who act on the progressive/statist premise in government.

205. (c) The universal class [the class of civil servants] has for its task the universal interests of the community. It must therefore be relieved from direct labor to supply its needs, either by having private means or by receiving an al-

lowance from the state, which claims its industry, with the result that private interest finds its satisfaction in its work for the universal. [18]

Hegel, Kant, Fichte, and Nietzsche helped to influence the nationalist movement that became the Second German empire. Once the empire was reestablished under Kaiser Wilhelm I, Chancellor Otto von Bismarck instituted significant social legislation "including the eight-hour work day, health care, social insurance, and the like. Bismarck's motive was to forestall demands for more democracy by giving the people the sort of thing they might ask for at the polls. His top-down socialism was a Machiavellian masterstroke, because it made the middle class dependent upon the state. The middle class took away from this the lesson that enlightened government was not the product of democracy but an alternative to it."[19]

At American colleges and universities, Hegel and German idealism increasingly influenced the history, government, and sociology faculties. This helped initiate the American progressive movement, which basically assumed the progressives could govern America better than the business leaders and capitalists, who were limited by the premises of the Declaration of Independence and the federal Constitution:

> By 1900, the faculties of American colleges and universities had become populated with European Ph.D.s and the historical thinking that dominated Europe (especially Germany) in the ninetieth century that came to permeate American higher education.[20]

Ronald Pestritto and William Atto wrote *American Progressivism*, and many of the subsequent quotations are taken from that work.

> Like their European counterparts, American Progressives championed *der Staat* over the individual, seeking to redistribute wealth and use the national government to su-

perintend society and the economy. ... reflecting on what it means to be a progressive, Wilson wrote of government as a "living thing", which was to be understood according to "the theory of organic life." This "living" notion of a constitution, Wilson contended, was far superior to the founders model, which had considered government a kind of machine that could be constantly limited through checks and balances. As a living entity, the progressives reasoned, government had to evolve and adapt in response to changing circumstances. While early American conceptions of national governments had carefully circumscribed its power due to the perceived threat to individual liberties, progressives argued that history had brought about an improvement in the human condition, such that the will of the people was no longer in danger of becoming factious.[21]

Jonah Goldberg wrote *Liberal Fascism*, which traces the intellectual roots of the progressive/statist agenda. He provides some additional insights into the thinking of Woodrow Wilson as a young professor of political science:

Woodrow Wilson's view of politics was shaped at Johns Hopkins University, where almost the entire fifty-three faculty members had been much influenced by German historicism. . . . Wilson's worldview could be summarized by the word "statolatry" or state worship. Wilson believed that the state was a natural, organic, and spiritual expression of the people themselves. From the outset, he believed that the government and people should have an organic bond that reflected the *Volksgeist* or the "true spirit" of the people.[22]

Wilson greatly admired Bismarck's welfare state as "an 'admirable system, the most studied and most nearly perfected' in the world. … Woodrow Wilson's most prominent and influential teacher was Richard Ely who taught his students to imagine a socialism of spirit that would replace laissez-faire from within men's hearts."[23]

In the late nineteenth century, many Americans in the growing middle class became concerned about government corruption and its failure to deal with urban and industrial problems. This Social Gospel movement contributed to the launching of the American progressive movement that called for the modernization and reform of decrepit institutions, the elimination of corruption in politics, and the introduction of efficiency as criteria for change. Beginning in the 1880s and lasting through the First World War, Social Gospel represented the response of liberal evangelical Protestantism to the intellectual challenges of Darwinism. Social Gospel theologians posited evolution as a divine plan for rational social advancement "thy will be done on earth as it is in heaven," and they asserted that government, because of progress, was now in a position to bring about such an earthly utopia in the form of the modern democratic state. As a practical matter, this meant overcoming man's attachment to private property, and removing private property rights as an obstacle to social action.[24]

As the nineteenth century closed with a sparkling list of technological achievements, there was opportunity for millions from all over who came to the US to start a new life. The solid structure provided by the Founding Fathers in the Declaration of Independence ("apple of gold") and the Constitution ("frame of silver") were under scrutiny as obstacles to achieve social justice and the redistribution of wealth. The American progressive movement had been spawned with its underlying premise of statism. In the next chapter, the full impact of this effort to overcome conservative constitutionalism will be explained.

2. THE PROGRESSIVE MOVEMENT AND ERODING THE FEDERAL CONSTITUTION

Teddy Roosevelt, a hero of the Spanish American War became the first unofficial progressive president in 1901. Then, in a three-way 1912 election, Woodrow Wilson was the first authentic progressive president. Thereafter, a concerted progressive/statist erosion of the federal Constitution commenced from 1913 through 2009. Today, there is an Iron Triangle – comprised of politicians, bureaucrats and beneficiaries of government programs.

The American Progressive Movement

Pestritto and Atto provide the following summary definition of progressivism:

> Progressivism is an argument to progress, or to move beyond, the political principles of the American founding. It is an argument to enlarge vastly the scope of national government for the purpose of responding to a set of economic and social conditions which, progressives contend, could not have been envisioned at the founding and for which the founders' limited, constitutional government was inadequate. Whereas the founders had posited what they held to be a permanent understanding of just government, based

upon a permanent account of human nature, the progressives countered that the ends and scope of government were to be defined anew in each historical epoch. They coupled this perspective of historical contingency with a deep faith in historical progress, suggesting that, due to historical evolution, government was becoming less of a danger to the governed and more capable of solving the great array of problems besetting the human race.[1]

Many of the academic progressives saw that empowering expert administrators would be the way to achieve progress in solving industrial and urban problems:

American government needed to be reformed so that it reflected the essential unity of the public mind that progressives believed had been brought about by history. Separation of powers … had to be replaced by a system that instead separated politics and administration. At the same time, the real work of government was not in politics, but in administration—in figuring out the specific means of achieving what the people generally agreed they all wanted. … At a more general level, the real problem, as progressives saw it, was a failure of the courts to see the Constitution as a "living" organism, one whose limitations on government ought not be read strictly or literally, but instead interpreted to fit the new demands of a new age. … American government needed to be reformed so that it reflected the essential unity of the public mind that progressives believed had been brought about by history.[2]

Both as a professor and later as president, Woodrow Wilson advocated keeping the administration of government separate and distinct from politics. Pestritto and Atto summarized his views:

Wilson pioneered the separating administration from politics—in a series of essays in the 1880s. In the traditional view, administration was confined to the executive branch. It was thus confined to the exercise of executive power. Progressive administration, by contrast, was to be liberated from the influence of partisan or electoral politics and was to engage not only in executive action, but legislative and judicial as well. Administrators, on the basis of their expertise, would need to make rules and regulations, enforce them, and adjudicated violations of them. …The role that progressives had in mind for the national government greatly exceeded the capabilities of the traditional constitutional branches. And so the establishment of a substantial bureaucratic apparatus, largely free from the influence of electoral politics, not only became a means of facilitating government by educated experts, but also provided an institutional machinery that could take on many new tasks that progressives had in mind for the national government.[3]

Progressives believed that administrators, unlike politicians, could be objective and could focus on the good of the whole people—their ability to do so rested primarily on being freed from electoral accountability. The salary and life tenure of administrators would take care of any self-interested inclinations that might otherwise corrupt their decision-making.[4]

Political commentator and syndicated columnist George Will made this observation about the implementation of a government by administrators:

Woodrow Wilson said that the Princeton he led as its president was dedicated to unbiased expertise, and he thought government could be "reduced to science." Because they are entirely public-spirited, progressives volunteer to be the administrators, and to be as "disinterested as the dickens"… Wilson was the first president to criticize the Founding Fathers. He faulted them for designing a government too susceptible to factions that impeded disinterested experts from getting on with government business.[5]

What is significant to remember is that for the first time open and direct criticism of the Constitution occurred with the academic advocates of progressivism. Pestritto and Atto explain as follows:

> The Progressive Era was the first time in American political development to feature open and direct criticism of the Constitution. … They also knew that the limits placed on the national government by the Constitution represented major obstacles to implementing the progressive agenda. … The Constitution, if interpreted and applied faithfully, stood in the way of this agenda.[6]

Because they believe in historical progress, progressives argue that America no longer has to obsess over the subject of tyranny or the superstition of evil. Mankind is good; it is circumstances that cause men to behave in ways that are seen as selfish, greedy, rapacious, and even vicious. "For Wilson, the separation of powers had come out of the founders' obsessive fear of majority tyranny, and thus the system was outdated for the present age, where the people were no longer a danger to themselves."[7] In his essay on *Taming Big Government*, Michael Uhlmann provides this insight about the unintended consequences of Wilson's actions: "Wilson dealt the separation of powers a mortal blow without understanding the full implications of what he had wrought."[8]

Spanish-American War, Teddy Roosevelt, and the 1912 Election

The Spanish-American war was a result of an ongoing rebellion in Cuba. William Randolph Hearst and Joseph Pulitzer printed sensationalized "yellow journalism" stories about Spanish atrocities in Cuba. On February 15, 1898, the *USS Maine* exploded mysteriously in Havana Harbor. Spain declared war on the United States on April 24. Theodore Roosevelt abandoned his civilian position with the Navy, joined the Army, raised a cavalry regiment, and led his Rough Riders in the capture of San Juan Hill, which made him famous. When the American fleet destroyed Spain's Caribbean fleet on July 7, Spain signed an armistice. Under the terms of the Treaty of Paris, the United States annexed the islands of Puerto Rico, Guam, and the Philippines.

In the presidential election of 1900, President William McKinley chose Teddy Roosevelt as his running mate and was reelected to a second term. An anarchist shot McKinley on September 6, 1901. Roosevelt then became the twenty-fifth president of the United States, and, at age forty-three, the youngest ever to hold the office. He initiated a policy of increased federal enforcement of antitrust laws and supervision of the railroads.

In the 1904 election, Roosevelt was elected president in his own right. Roosevelt proved to be a dynamic president who crusaded for pure food laws, busted up trusts, and lobbied for still more drastic railroad regulation. Roosevelt made preservation of the nation's natural resources a high priority, and he called for a far-reaching and integrated program of conservation, reclamation, and irrigation. Roosevelt's conception of the presidency represented a novelty in the American political tradition. In his "Stewardship" theory, Roosevelt posited the idea that presidential power is not confined by the enumerated grants of power made in the Constitution:

> "I declined to adopt the view that what was imperatively necessary for the Nation could not be done by the President unless he could find some specific authorization to do it. My belief was that it was not only his right but his duty to do anything that the needs of the nation demanded unless such action was forbidden by the Constitution or by the laws." Teddy Roosevelt thus understood the powers of the national government, and especially those of the president, as *plenary,* not *enumerated*—defined, in other words,

by the needs of time, not by the provisions of Article II.
The president was to become the interpreter of the nation's
needs and was to use his position as the people's steward to
keep government responsive to those needs as they evolved
from one epoch to the next. It was in this way that the
presidency became, for progressives, the agent of progress
in national politics. [9]

Of course Roosevelt's attitude toward the presidency is a complete
departure from reality, because the federal government was designed as a
limited government with enumerated powers. In 1903, Congress created
a new cabinet department, Commerce and Labor. This is the first instance
where two economic interest groups—business and labor—received federal recognition. The second step of this erosion of the federal Constitution
occurred in 1913, when Congress split off the labor responsibility into a
new, separate cabinet department.

Roosevelt's popularity was at its peak in 1908, but he was unwilling
to break the tradition of no president holding office for more than two
terms. Roosevelt supported William Howard Taft who was elected president in 1908. During the next four years, President Taft pursued policies
that alienated the progressive wing of the Republican Party. Roosevelt's
dissatisfaction with Taft's handling of the presidency prompted him and his
supporters to form a third party, and Roosevelt became the 1912 nominee
of the Progressive Party (also known as the Bull Moose Party.)

Progressives championed a form of constitutionalism that
would be more immediately responsive to the rule of the
people. ... The Progressive program seemed to challenge
the very foundation of republican democracy: the idea,
underlying the U. S. Constitution, that space created by
institutional devices such as the separation of powers and
federalism allowed representatives to govern competently
and fairly. [10]

In 1912 election, Democrat Woodrow Wilson, then governor of New Jersey, opposed both Taft and Roosevelt. In the election Roosevelt split the votes sufficiently with Taft to cede the election to Wilson. With hindsight, this election can be regarded as a threshold election. "For better or worse, the progressive democracy championed by T.R. in 1912, and the love-hate relationship with the state it has led to, now seem enduring parts of our political life."[11]

The Progressive/Statist Erosion of the US Constitution

This section examines fourteen events that have chipped away at the rock of the US Constitution over the past one hundred years, from 1913 to 2012:

Chip No. 1: Enacting a federal income tax. When the idea of taxing the rich became sufficiently popular, a national income tax was put in place by the Sixteenth Amendment to the federal Constitution. "Once inaugurated, he moved to reduce the tariff, and, the lost revenues were to be recovered by making use of the recently ratified Sixteenth Amendment that levied an income tax on the wealthiest Americans."[12]

Chip No. 2: Direct election of senators. The Seventeenth Amendment, ratified in 1913, mandated the direct election of US senators by the people, replacing the prior system established in the original Constitution under which they were selected by state legislatures. This effectively diminished the role of the states as an impediment against future federal encroachment on individual liberties. When World War I broke out in 1914, the British established a crushing blockade, causing great hardship and suffering among German civilians. Germany retaliated against the blockade with U-boats. When the British passenger ship *Lusitania* was sunk without warning on May 15, 1915, and there were American casualties, anti-German feeling reached a high point in the United States. Germany promised not to repeat such an atttack.

In 1916 Wilson was reelected over Charles Evans Hughes, the Republican candidate, on a promise to keep America out of the war. The German High Command decided once again to pursue unrestricted U-boat warfare against all ships headed to Britain. This prompred Wilson to ask Congress for a declaration of war on April 6, 1917, despite his election promise. This experience of World War I created an enlarged centralized government. An entire array of new federal boards and commissions were established to deal with these new realities. In the summer of 1918, fresh American troops played a central role in the Allied final offensive. Victory was achieved when an armistice was declared on November 11, 1918.

In 1919 Wilson went to Europe as the primary architect of the League of Nations, which he said would prevent future wars of such magnitude through negotiation and arbitration. Wilson was forced into many compromises on outstanding issues with Germany until only the League of Nations was left. When Wilson returned home, the Republican majority in the Senate killed the treaty that would have required American participation in the League. Four million American soldiers returned from Europe with little planning, little money, and few benefits. A wartime bubble of farmland prices burst, leaving many farmers bankrupt or deeply in debt. Major strikes in steel, coal, and meatpacking followed in 1919. Serious race riots hit Chicago, Omaha, and two dozen other cities.

Chip No. 3: Prohibition. Another plank of the progressive platform was temperance, restricting the use of alcoholic beverages in an attempt to curtail the problem of alcoholism. Thus, for the first time, the Constitution was amended by the Eighteenth Amendment on January 16, 1919, for the purpose of regulating morality. This established prohibition, which criminalized the sale, manufacture, or transportation of alcoholic beverages. But the demand for beer and hard liquor continued unabated, and the police, courts, and prisons were overwhelmed with new cases. Organized crime increased in power, and corruption grew among law enforcement officials. Prohibition was an infringement upon the rights of the majority of Americans. The amendment was repealed in 1933 by ratification of the Twenty-first Amendment—the only time in United States history when a constitutional amendment was repealed.

Passage of the Nineteenth Amendment on August 26, 1920, was an affirmation of the "apple of gold" that asserts that all men and women are created equal and have natural rights to life, liberty, and the pursuit of happiness. The women's suffrage movement that began in 1848 finally realized its goal when Wilson urged Congress to pass a Constitutional amendment enfranchising women. Because of the Nineteenth Amendment, American women cast their votes for the first time in the 1920 election. The Republicans chose Warren Harding of Ohio with Calvin Coolidge as his running mate, and they soundly defeated Democratic nominees James Cox and Franklin Roosevelt.

The Roaring Twenties were known as the Jazz Age because of the popularity of jazz music and the excessive consumption of illegal alcohol. Harding and Coolidge ushered in a period of national prosperity by lowering income taxes. Harding died on August 2, 1923, and was replaced by Coolidge, who faced problems in the Midwest, where many farmers in the Dust Bowl had to sell out and move to other places, especially California. Herbert Hoover was elected president in 1928, and the artificial prosperity of the stock market was shattered by a massive sell off of stocks on Black Thursday, October 24, 1929. By 1932 millions were out of work. In the election of 1932, Democratic nominee Franklin D. Roosevelt pledged a New Deal for the American people and was swept into office over Hoover. "European-style statism took greater hold over the country through FDR's New Deal. Roosevelt was no intellectual but he relied on his progressive and fascist predecessors for the model of state power that animated his programs."[13]

Chip No. 4: The New Deal's regulatory agencies. During Roosevelt's first hundred days, he instituted a number of new agencies and policies, including the National Recovery Administration; the Civilian Conservation Corps; the Agricultural Adjustment Act; the Works Progress Administration; the Public Works Administration; the Federal Art Project; the Tennessee Valley Authority; and many others. [14] The net consequence of creating all these agencies in the name of a national emergency was to go beyond the enumerated powers of the federal government and to encroach upon the powers reserved to the people and to the states by the Ninth and Tenth amendments.

Chip No. 5: Intimidating the US Supreme Court. After his reelection in 1936, with growing unemployment and continuing misery in the agricultural states, FDR generated much animosity by proposing changes to the Supreme Court appointment process. This was consistent with the progressive (statist) view that dispersed power was inefficient and centralized power was needed to accomplish good works for the citizens. "In the progressive view, intentions and sincerity are among the noblest virtues a president can possess. Experimentation is valued more than experience, and compassion, not results, is described as 'the best answer.'"[15] As a consequence of FDR's intimidation, the US Supreme Court has tended to make more use of the "living Constitution" idea advocated by the progressive/statist agenda.

Chip No. 6: A president as the national leader. It was only after decades of struggle that a new constitutional order, with the president as its driving force, came to ultimate fruition in the New Deal. The nation's chief executive would defeat the original Constitution's structural obstacles by rising above them. Wilson's chosen instrument for this purpose was party government, which would breach the parchment barriers dividing president and Congress and unite both through a common policy agenda initiated by the president. The president would make the case for policy innovation directly to the people. Once armed with authority direct from the voters (plebisictary legitimacy), he might more easily prod an otherwise stuck-in-the mud (parochial) Congress to address national needs. Congress and the president would jointly settle upon the desired policy agendas, but its details, both in design and execution, would rely on non-partisan expert administrators' special insight and technical skill, operating under the president's general direction and control. The presidency, thus reconceived, would by turns become a voice for and dominant instrument of a reconceived federal Constitution, which would at last detach itself from a foolish preoccupation with limited government. The appearance of a constitutional republic would become the false front for an underlying reality of a progressive/statist agenda in operation:

The old Constitution's formal structure would be retained, insofar as that might be politically necessary; but it would be essentially emptied of its prior substantive content. The president (would now be seen) as proactive government's innovator-in-chief, one who was best positioned to understand historical tendencies and to unite them with popular yearnings. In an almost mystical sense, the president would embody the will of the people, becoming both prophet and steward of a new kind of egalitarian *Manifest Destiny* at home and in the fullness of time, perhaps throughout the world.[16]

After the outbreak of World War II in 1939, Roosevelt was reelected in 1940 to a third consecutive term, which broke the tradition established by George Washington. On a "date that will live in infamy," December 7, 1941, the Japanese military government launched a surprise attack against the US Navy base at Pearl Harbor.

Chip No. 7: A Congress regulating intrastate commerce. In a decision that should be regarded as the most disastrous since the *Dred Scott* decision of 1857, during World War II, enmeshed in the attitudes of trying to correct a massive economic dislocation caused by the Great Depression, the US Supreme Court decided to uphold the authority of Congress to regulate intrastate, as distinguished from interstate, commerce. The case concerned a wheat farmer who was growing wheat only for his own use and who did not to engage in sale across state lines. "What makes that 1942 case—*Wickard v. Filburn*—important today is that it stretched the federal government's power so far that the Obama administration is using it before today's Supreme Court as an argument to claim that it has the legal authority to impose Obamacare mandates on individuals."[17]

Unless this national healthcare decision is overturned, it will effectively emasculate the federalism established by the Tenth Amendment and the powers that are reserved for the states. Further, it makes mockery of the enumerated powers intended in the federal Constitution by the Founding Fathers.

Franklin Roosevelt applied the progressive/statist agenda to expand the role of government in American society. In 1944, Roosevelt announced a so-called second bill of rights. Burton Folsom, in *New Deal or Raw Deal? How FDR's Economic Legacy Has Damaged America,* summarizes the new rights announced by FDR:

> Roosevelt conceded that the United States "grew to its present strength under the protection of certain inalienable political rights" but then argued that "these political rights proved inadequate to assure us equality in the pursuit of happiness." In 1944, he elaborated an *Economic Bill of Rights* that included "the right to a useful and remunerative job; the right of every family to a decent home; the right to a good education." . . . Roosevelt's new progressive rights, unlike those of the founders, imposed obligations on society to provide jobs, buy homes, and pay for educations. Government, by necessity, had to increase in size to tax some citizens to provide newly discovered "rights" for others. Where the Founders wanted government limited mainly to protect rights, Roosevelt and the progressives wanted expanded government to provide jobs, recreation, education and houses. Where the Founders were skeptical of human nature, the progressives were optimistic that a president, or a small group of administrators, could use government to create the good life for Americans and preserve liberty as well. Results, in Roosevelt's view, were more important than process; intentions more important than protecting natural rights; plans and new ideas more important than experience.[18]

The American Navy turned the tide of war with a crucial victory in the Battle of Midway (June 4-7, 1942). In the largest amphibious invasion ever, American, British, and Canadian troops landed in France on D-Day, June 6, 1944. American and Japanese naval forces fought what is generally considered the largest naval battle in all of military history: the Battle of Leyte Gulf, on October 23-26, 1944. Running for an unprecedented fourth term, Roosevelt defeated Thomas Dewey in 1944. This action prompted the Constitution to work properly, for an amendment to the Constitution—number twenty-two—was adopted on February 27, 1951, limiting election to the office to no more than two terms. On April 12, 1945, Roosevelt died, and Vice President Harry S. Truman, a World War I veteran, became president. The Soviet and Allied forces forced Germany to surrender, ending World War II in Europe on May 8, 1945. The United Nations charter was signed, carrying forward Wilson's idea of the League of Nations but without explicit war powers.

Anticipating the probability of more than a million casualties in an attempt to invade Japan, Truman approved dropping the first atomic bombs on Hiroshima and Nagasaki, Japan. With the first use of these most devastating weapons, mankind crossed into a nuclear age in which the power existed to obliterate all human life from the earth. Japan surrendered on September 2, 1945, bringing World War II to an end. Not only had millions of fighting forces died but also millions of innocent civilians. Following World War II, millions enrolled in college under the GI bill. This kept them off the labor market for several years; an unintended consequence was the overabundance of college-educated people who disdained manual labor and sought white-collar careers instead. This was the pool from which an increasing number of individuals took positions in government—appointed and elected—that are now part of the Cognoscenti.

In 1946 the Cold War with the Soviet Union commenced. The world's two remaining superpowers threatened each other for more than forty-five years and viewed the rest of the world in terms of their confrontation. On June 25, 1950, communist North Korea invaded South Korea. The United Nations voted to intervene on behalf of South Korea. The United Nations forces, led by five-star General Douglas MacArthur, drove the North Korean communists back to the border of China, provoking a massive Chinese counterattack. Because of a difference of opinion on the use of the atomic bomb, Truman correctly fulfilled his role as civilian commander- in- chief and fired MacArthur. Both sides in the Korean War agreed to an armistice in 1953, and that has been the war's official status ever since. In 1952 five-star General Dwight Eisenhower was elected president over Adlai Stevenson, grandson of a former vice president.

Chip No. 8: More federal intrusion into areas reserved for the states. Eisenhower created the Health and Human Services Department on March 12, 1953. This furthered the progressive/statist agenda of allowing the federal government to encroach upon health and education services that previously were the sole province of the states. Unfortunately, with the reality of federal income tax collections, money first flowed to Washington, DC, and then was disbursed by the Cognoscenti back to the states in the form of grants- in-aid and student loans.

The world changed again when the USSR successfully launched Sputnik on October 4, 1957, the start of the Space Age. In the 1960 election, John F. Kennedy was elected president over Vice President Richard Nixon—the first Roman Catholic to hold the office. In the 1960s, the civil rights movement continued and expanded. In the new television age, Americans witnessed dramatic and brave acts to secure civil rights as people were beaten and hosed but kept on with the struggle.

After the US broke diplomatic relations with Cuba, an attempted invasion to oust the Castro government—the Bay of Pigs invasion—turned into a disaster for lack of American air and naval support. This made Kennedy and the Americans appear weak to the Soviets, and they responded by constructing the Berlin Wall. In 1962 the Soviet Union attempted to install intercontinental ballistic missiles in Cuba, only ninety miles from the US shoreline. Kennedy ordered a blockade of Cuba, which became known as the Cuban Missile Crisis when it appeared that nuclear war might break out. Fortunately both sides agreed to back down gracefully.

To help the beleaguered South Vietnamese government, President Kennedy authorized sending over Army Special Forces. In South Vietnam, a military coup overthrew President Diem who was assassinated on November 3, 1963. A few weeks later, on November 22, Americans learned the stunning news of the assassination of President Kennedy. For the eighth time in American history, the vice president—this time Lyndon Johnson—was elevated upon the death of an incumbent president.

Chip No. 9: Without a formal declaration of war, the Vietnam War commenced. The US destroyer *Maddox* was allegedly attacked in the Gulf of Tonkin, South Vietnam, in August 1964. The Constitution makes the Congress responsible for declaring war. Inspired by the uncertainties of the Cold War with the Soviet Union, Congress decided to delegate to President Johnson the authority to use all power necessary to repel attacks on US forces. This resolution became the basis for intervention by US military forces in Vietnam. In the 1964 election, President Lyndon Johnson routed Senator Barry Goldwater, who was portrayed as a war hawk. In 1965, due to a massive escalation of the US military effort in Vietnam and nightly TV coverage of it, antiwar demonstrations became widespread. A majority of the American people reacted.

> What did the average workingman have in common with hippies who spent their time taking drugs and squandering their families' trust funds? Or with students who desecrated the American flag? The antiwar protesters, most of whom would be given student deferments rather than being sent to fight, were even more unpopular than the war itself.[19]

Medgar Evers was shot and killed on June 12, 1963. Malcolm X was shot and killed on February 21, 1965. Author Ben Stein gives us this perspective:

> Blacks were still being killed in the South, and the outrage of the nation inspired President Lyndon Johnson to urge passage of the Civil Rights Act of 1964 (and) the Voting Rights Act of 1965. What's vital to remember is that when we see the films of demonstrators marching back then, there are almost always large numbers of white people present along with the blacks.... Try to imagine this in another country.[20]

Chip No. 10 The Great Society and the creation of two new federal departments. President Johnson launched Great Society programs that included the Voting Rights Act, added to the Civil Rights Act; a declaration of war on poverty; the Head Start program; and the enormous Medicare and Medicaid programs. Many of these were undoubtedly laudable, but even the best policies can have unintended consequences. Two more departments were created as further encroachments into areas of responsibility reserved for the states—the Department of Housing and Urban Development and the Department of Transportation. "(These Great Society programs) built up a dynamic of their own, throwing up bureaucratic empires and stoking white resentment. And they relentlessly dragged the Democratic Party ever further from its centrist roots, swelling the 'coalition of the fed-up' that had voted for Goldwater. The Democrats' civil rights agenda rapidly broadened from guaranteeing basic rights to black citizens (such as the right to equal opportunity and to vote) to making amends for past injustices with preferential treatment."[21]

Jonah Goldberg makes an important point about how the Cognoscenti use the war metaphor in order to rally support for new programs:

> The chief appeal of war to social planners isn't conquest or death but mobilization.… War brings conformity and unity of purpose. The ordinary rules of behavior are mothballed. You can get things done: build roads, hospitals, and houses. Domestic populations and institutions were required to "do their part"… Hence, in more recent times, the left has looked to everything from environmentalism and global warming to public health and "diversity" as war equivalents to cajole the public into expert-driven unity.[22]

> Johnson's Great Society, with its War on Poverty, expansion of federal government responsibilities and programs, higher income taxes, and commitment to ending segregation in the public sector and enforcing the right to vote, sought to transform American politics in ways never before

attempted by the National Democratic Party. Many Southern whites interpreted these developments as direct attacks on their interests and traditions. Johnson's decisive shift to the left broke the ties that bound many conservative Southern whites to the Democratic Party. [23]

All the while the country was falling apart. The North Vietnamese launched the Tet Offensive (January-February 1968). Tactically they lost the battles; strategically they convinced the American public that the war was unwinable. The public outcry over the war convinced President Johnson not to run for reelection. In the 1968 election, Richard Nixon prevailed over Vice President Hubert Humphrey. "Nixon ruthlessly used cultural issues to drive a wedge between working-class Democrats and their increasingly liberal party."[24] Jonah Goldberg compares and contrasts the progressive/statist expansion that occurred under presidents Kennedy and Johnson:

> Most historians view Kennedy and Johnson as ending the era that began with Wilson and ran through the New Deal and the Fair Deal to the New Frontier and the Great Society. But the Kennedy presidency marked the final evolution of Progressivism into a full-blown religion and a national cult of the state. John F. Kennedy represented the cult of personality tradition of American Liberalism. Lyndon Baines Johnson, a southern populist ward heeler could neither be a warrior nor a priest. He could embody the maternal aspect of Progressivism as the caring a protective shepherd overseeing his flock. ... His legacy, the modern welfare state, represents the ultimate fruition of a progressive statist tradition going back to Woodrow Wilson. [25]

Chip No. 11: Nixon continues the progressive/statist agenda with the creation of more Federal agencies. President Nixon created several new government agencies that conservatives would spend much of the next two decades trying to get rid of: the Environmental Protection Agency and the Occupational Safety and Health Administration. Nixon particularly infuriated conservatives by creating the Cost of Living Council in 1971-73 to try to control prices and wages.

In the 1972 election, Nixon was reelected over George McGovern. Then, in October 1973, Spiro Agnew became the first man to resign as vice-president because of criminal charges, and Gerald Ford was appointed to replace him. Because of the Watergate scandal and possibility of impeachment, Richard Nixon became the first president to resign on August 9, 1974. Ford became the only man to serve both as vice president and president without being elected by the Electoral College.

The number of American soldiers in Vietnam rose from 23,300 in 1963 to 542,000 by January 1969. Despite this size, and micromanaging from Washington, DC, the US Army was unable to subdue Vietnam. American military forces were withdrawn in 1973, and the communist North Vietnamese conquered South Vietnam in 1975. Vietnam was our first military defeat in an overseas war. In the 1976 election, Georgia Governor Jimmy Carter prevailed over Ford.

Chip No. 12: The progressive/statist agenda advanced by creating two more federal departments. Carter created the Energy Department in October 1977 and the Education Department in 1979. The latter was split off from Health and Human Services and controlled the flow of money to what was once the sole prerogative of the states and local government. Then the revolutionary movement in Teheran attacked the American embassy and took hostages. Carter's administration was frustrated, unable to rescue the hostages, and unwilling to go to war for fear of starting World War III with the Soviet Union. In the 1980 election, former California Governor Ronald Reagan prevailed over Carter.

Ronald Reagan rode into the White House on a wave of conservative resentment against "big government," the United States had a lower tax rate, a smaller deficit as a proportion of GNP, a less developed welfare state and fewer government-owned industries than any other western industrialized nation. [26]

During Reagan's inauguration, Iran released the hostages it had imprisoned for a total of 444 days. During his first term in office, Reagan pushed through significant tax cuts to stimulate the economy and reduce the nation's high inflation and rate of unemployment. In 1984 Ronald Reagan was reelected over Senator Walter Mondale. In a series of meetings with Mikhail Gorbachev, the Soviet premier, Reagan told him America would build an antiballistic missile shield. In the face of Reagan's firmness, Gorbachev realized the USSR did not have the economic resources to keep up the arms race with America. This set changes in motion and eventually led to the collapse of the Soviet Union.

In the 1988 election, Vice President George H. W. Bush prevailed over Massachusetts Governor Michael Dukakis. President Bush faced the reality of a swollen national debt caused by spending and borrowing to defeat the Soviet Union in the arms race. He was forced into raising taxes, and that action later doomed his chances for reelection.

Chip No. 13: Creation of another federal department. The progressive/statist agenda was advanced again with the creation of the federal Veterans Affairs Department in March 15, 1989. Certainly Congress has control over all military expenditures, however, elevating this administrative service function to cabinet level has to be viewed as a political move that focuses on a particular voting constituency. The massive numbers of employees in the federal government continues to reinforce the power and control sought by the Cognoscenti.

Saddam Hussein invaded Kuwait in August 1990; in response President Bush formed a United Nations coalition that quickly routed the Iraqi army out of Kuwait (the first Gulf war, 1990-1991). After a hard-line communist coup against Mikhail Gorbachev failed in August 1991, the Union of Soviet Socialist Republics was formally dissolved and replaced by the Confederation of Independent States on December 21, 1991. Gorbachev resigned and Boris Yeltsin became president of the Russian Confederation, marking the end to the forty-six years of the Cold War.

In the 1992 election, Ross Perot took enough votes away from President Bush to give the election to Arkansas Governor Bill Clinton, who routed Bush by promising a more active government. In 1994 a Republican majority in the House forced through welfare reform and a balanced budget.

> The contract with America, compiled by the congressional Republicans, was an extraordinary document—a list of ten policy proposals that received the support of more than three hundred GOP candidates and ended with the promise: "If we break this contract, throw us out"… In August 1996, the Republicans sent an unadulterated welfare-reform bill to the president—and dared him to sign it… Clinton signed it—and thus sealed one of the great conservative achievements of his presidency. By 2000, there were 7.5 million fewer people on welfare.[27]

In the 1996 election, President Clinton prevailed over Kansas Senator Robert Dole. Clinton's second term was marred by the Monica Lewinsky scandal and an attempt by the congressional Republicans to impeach Clinton for lying under oath.

Chip No. 14: The Supreme Court forced into deciding the 2000 election.

In the 2000 election, Vice President Al Gore lost to Governor George W. Bush. This required the US Supreme Court to make what was perceived as a political decision by the losing side. The court declared George W. Bush president over Al Gore on December 12, 2000. The results of the election in 2000 turned on 537 votes out of 5,963,110 cast in Florida. "Al Gore's defeat in the 2000 election is one of liberal America's horror stories, because, Gore lost an election that he should have won in a walk."[28]

The threat of radical Islamist terrorism was made manifest on American soil by the destruction of the World Trade Center towers on September 11, 2001. President Bush retaliated with invasions of Afghanistan and Iraq. In the 2004 election, President Bush prevailed over Massachusetts Senator John Kerry. Both Hurricane Katrina and financial meltdowns occurred during Bush's second term.

In the 2008 election, Illinois Senator Barack Obama prevailed over Arizona Senator John McCain. In a history-making event, Barack Obama became the first biracial American elected as chief executive. In 2008 the American republic could celebrate 220 years of constitutional government. However, as noted above, the desire to have economic protection provided by the government has implemented a progressive/statist agenda that has the potential to irrevocably erode American individual liberties. The massive centralization of the federal government caused by these chippings away of the US Constitution has enormously increased the numbers employed in government. This gives rise to an ongoing problem that will be discussed next: the "iron triangle".

The Iron Triangle—Politicians, Bureaucrats, and Beneficiaries

From Woodrow Wilson to Barack Obama, more and more power and control has been concentrated in Washington, DC, thereby creating a multitude of new jobs in the federal bureaucracy. According to Milton Friedman, a Nobel economist and author of *Tyranny of the Status Quo*, there is now an "iron triangle" that has three corners—the elected politicians, the appointed bureaucrats, and the direct beneficiaries of laws and/or regulations.[29]

First there is the tyranny of the politicians. According to Judge Robert Bork, author of *Slouching Towards Gomorrah—Modern Liberalism and American Decline*, politicians identified with modern liberalism or the progressive/statist agenda include "most of the Democratic Congressional party, and some of the Republican Congressional party."[46] Ever since democratic government was established, those aspiring to be elected to public office have sought to buy votes. In the Roman republic, upon the death of Julius Caesar, Mark Antony famously promised a share of Caesar's inheritance to the populace. Friedman points out that traditionally votes are purchased with either a patron's or one's own money.

Since the 1930s, the technique of buying votes with the voters' own money has been expanded to an extent undreamed of by earlier politicians. ... The major way in which candidates buy votes with the voters' own money is very different—by promising all voters goodies supposedly to be paid for by other voters. ... Patrons remain important: the lobbyists, the political action committees, the various other kinds of special interest groups that provided campaign funds for candidates. ... Members of Congress now get much support from groups that seek either to have special benefits introduced into the tax system, or else to prevent benefits from being withdrawn, or finally to prevent special impositions from being levied on them.[30]

The only way for Congress to give one American a dollar is to first, through the tax code, take that dollar from some other American. It must forcibly use one American to serve another American. Forcibly using one person to serve another person is one way to describe slavery. As such, it violates self-ownership. Walter Williams summarizes how the power of elected politicians impacts America:

Supreme Court Justice Louis Brandeis warned, "The greatest dangers to liberty lurk in the insidious encroachment by men of zeal, well meaning but without understanding." The freedom of individuals from compulsion or coercion never was, and is not now, the normal state of human affairs. The normal state for the ordinary person is tyranny, arbitrary control and abuse mainly by their own government. While imperfect in its execution, the founders of our nation sought to make an exception to this ugly part of mankind's history. Unfortunately, at the urging of the American people, we are unwittingly in the process of returning to mankind's normal state of affairs. Americans demand that Congress spend trillions of dollars on farm subsidies, business bailouts, education subsidies, Social Security, Medicare and prescription drugs and other elements of a welfare state.... If the average American were asked whether he wishes to return to mankind's normal state of affairs featured by arbitrary abuse, control and government dictates, I am sure he would find such a suggestion repulsive.... The problem with congressmen producing favors and privileges to all interest groups is that it creates what none of us wants: massive control, numerous dictates and micromanagement of our lives. There is no question that if one were to ask whether we Americans are moving toward more liberty or more government control over our lives, the answer would unambiguously be the latter—more government control over our lives."[31]

Second, there is the tyranny of the bureaucracy. The actual conduct of government is delegated to bureaucrats, the number of which has grown immensely over the years. From 1933 to 1982, the population of the United States didn't quite double, but the total number of employees of the federal government multiplied almost fivefold. In addition hundreds of thousands, perhaps millions, of persons who are not listed as civilian employees of the federal government are employed as consultants, advisers on contract, and the like.

Every large bureaucracy, government or private, knows the way it conducts its affairs is the best way. "Diamonds may or may not be a girl's best friend, but a crisis is without doubt the surest ally a government can have. Without crises, we could almost forget the need for any government." The former chief of staff to President Obama, Rahm Emanuel, famously observed that "you never want a serious crisis to go to waste." As one example of not wasting a crisis, there is the US Department of Energy. "Consider the Energy Department, which has 16,000 employees and a budget of $34 billion. It was created to solve the energy chaos of the 1970s, which it failed to do.... Yet the bureaucracy lives on."[32]

An already large and unwieldy federal establishment, expanding to meet the rising expectations of an ever more demanding and dependent public, threatens to become yet larger, more powerful, and harder to control. But, despite what bureaucrats might wish to believe about the beneficial effects of their expertise, the administrative state is not a machine that can run itself. It requires coherent policy direction; it needs to be managed with reasonable efficiency; and it has to be held politically accountable. ... Modern congressional oversight has become an elaborate and sophisticated version of the old spoils system adapted to the machinery of the administrative state. There is enough boodle in a nearly $3 trillion federal budget to satisfy even the most rapacious pork-barreler. ... One may say by way of summary that Congress has, without fully realizing it, succumbed to Wilson's plan to eviscerate the separation of powers. It has failed to realize it in part because the administrative state's growth has occurred gradually; in part because it has learned how to profit politically by the change; and in part because it has convinced itself that conducting guerilla raids against executive authority is the most beneficial expression of the legislative function. [33]

As a former advisor in the Clinton White House and author of *2010 Take Back America*, Dick Morris has observed firsthand how the federal government operates from within. In particular he identifies bureaucracy as the oppressor and the most important adversary to our rights to liberty, property, and the pursuit of happiness:

Now after we faced and destroyed the demons of the twentieth century, we meet the greatest threat of all to our freedom at the outset of the twenty-first. The most potent adversary of democracy is bureaucracy. Bureaucracy offers us a vague promise: *Give us the power, take away our political constraints, let us rule, and we will do it right.* It plays on the same emotion as dictatorships do. It tells those who are fed up, fearful, and fatigued by politics to let the experts take over. ... Early in the century—when our ancestors were still naïve about civil service and saw "merit selection" as the alternative to patronage politics—some public policy commentators believed in the fantasy that the nation's business could best be conducted by administrators who would disregard politics and profit and make all the correct decisions for our country. But now, as we watch bureaucracy (and its handmaiden, public employee unionization) destroy one by one the institutions of our nation—the Post Office, the Veterans Hospitals, the public schools—we see the bureaucrat for what he is: our oppressor. [34]

Third, there is the tyranny of the beneficiaries. This is the most intractable and complex aspect of the iron triangle. If one adds up all the beneficiaries, it accounts for a majority of Americans. The three dominant patterns of benefiting from big government are employment, money payments, and preferential treatment.

Government employment—either working directly for the government or working for an organization that depends upon government contracts—now encompasses half of all adult employment in America. In part the American economy consists mainly of jobholders. As noted by Williams, who was quoted above, "the freedom of individuals from compulsion or coercion never was, and is not now, the normal state of human affairs. The normal state for the ordinary person is tyranny, arbitrary control and abuse mainly by their own government."

When common people could work a farm or tend a herd, they could take care of themselves economically. It was easy enough to submit to some form of tyranny in order to gain safety and protection from invaders. Now, however, those who actually labor to produce foodstuffs are in a minority. Thus, in addition to needing safety protections, we now seek economic protection from the normal ups and downs of a market economy. Government has created safety nets—unemployment insurance, welfare, Social Security, Medicare, and so forth. The biggest source of economic protection is the perceived security of government employment because there is no worry about being laid off.

Government disbursement of monetary payments is becoming ever more pervasive. In addition to the entitlement programs mentioned above, there are many other government payments, including veterans' benefits, Social Security disability payments, Medicaid, and income tax credits to those who qualify below a certain level.

The most traditional form of government benefits are those seeking preferential treatment. This can be in the form of direct subsidies to enhance one's economic advantage, such as tariffs on imports. Or it can be in the form of licensing requirements to reduce the competition from alternative competitors. As observed by Williams:

> There were nearly 35,000 highly paid registered lobbyists in Washington in 2004 who spent $2.1 billion lobbying the White House, Congress and various agencies on behalf of various interest groups. Political action committees, private donors and companies give billions of dollars to political campaigns. … For the most part, the money is being spent to get politicians and government officials to use their coercive power to create a favor or special privilege for one American at the expense of some other American. [35]

Once these programs are in place, it becomes extraordinarily difficult to reduce or eliminate them. I had the experience of seeing a county government in California try to eliminate a part-time position that administered benefits for veterans. On the day of the hearing, the chambers were filled with veterans wearing their white, World War II-style caps; some also wore medals. Most of them spoke against the proposal. Of course the board of supervisors caved in to this pressure and voted to retain the position. Writing in the 1960s, Friedman explained the inverse relationship between those who benefit from a program and those who are concerned about the costs of maintaining the program:

> With a typical government program, the persons who initially receive the benefits from a program are typically not the persons who would currently be harmed by its elimination. One group benefits when the program is first instituted; a different group is hurt if and when it is terminated. … (In a wide set of examples:) ICC restrictions on trucking and busing, CAB restrictions on airlines, FCC controls on television, radio and telephone; price ceilings on crude oil and natural gas; licensing of occupations; rent controls; agricultural price supports, tariffs and import quotas, etc.— all are cases of private wealth created by measures that harm the public. … Under these circumstances, it is not hard to see why there is a tyranny of beneficiaries, why it is so much harder to dismantle a program than it is to put a new one in place.[36]

Whenever an institution accepts government largesse, it is no longer in the business of profit making. Instead politicians and bureaucrats are eager to use the institutions they saved as social concepts meant to hand out non-economic loans, hire based on gender or race, and forgive non-performing loans. Banks sought government security in 2008 and they face much worse times ahead as the same government seeks payback in the form of coerced business activity that has nothing to do with profit. Consider how the support of family farms has transformed itself into a huge form of crony capitalism.

> When the U. S. bailed out the agriculture sector in the early 1930s, it forever changed the business of farming. … "Emergency" depression-era measures meant to protect farming families from short-term market swings have become near-permanent support at taxpayer expense.… Con-

gress stresses the romance of the family farm, but their fog of sentimentality obscures pertinent facts: 57% of farms receive no payments and two-thirds of those that do receive less than $10,000. The largest 8% of the farms receive 58% of the payments. Farms with revenue of $250,000 or more receive payments averaging $70,000. ... Under the continuing New Deal approach, five commodities—corn, soybeans, cotton, rice and wheat—got about 90% of last year's $19 billion in subsidies. [37]

Two commentators on the abuses in government programs are Robert Samuelson and John Stossel:

There is often a life cycle in government programs. They may start with good intentions, then perpetuate themselves by creating a protective web of interests—constituents who believe they have property rights in benefits, politicians whose power derives from renewing or expanding the benefits, and lobbies that exist to influence crucial politicians. Farm programs adhere faithfully to this cycle. FDR and Congress pass the Agricultural Adjustment Act (AAA) on May 12, 1938. ... The AAA empowered the government to control crop production and pay farmers to limit plantings.... The AAA made stabilizing farmers' incomes a political matter. Most of today's farm programs are simply transfers from consumers and taxpayers to farmers.[38]

The Patriot Act was supposed to provide federal funding to states to equip the fire, police, and EMS officers who serve at the front lines of a terrorist attack. But the Congressmen who wrote the law apparently believed that patriotism starts at home. Money was allocated under such a complicated formula where each state, regardless of its size or location, got an equal slice of the pie before risk was even considered.[39]

Politicians wanted to appeal for votes to low-income folk who did not own homes. So financial institutions received various types of pressure to relax lending requirements so every American could enjoy a right to home ownership. Williams accurately described the consequences of this politically motivated program:

> Most of the greatest problems we face are caused by politicians creating solutions to problems they created in the first place. ... The Community Reinvestment Act of 1977 encouraged banks and thrifts to make so-called "no doc" and "liar" loans to customers who had no realistic ability to pay them back. ... Government actions helped create the sub prime crisis, and now government-proposed solutions, such as foreclosure holidays, bailouts and further regulation of financial institutions, for the problems government created will create more problems.[40]

Thomas Sowell similarly observed the consequences of government intrusion into the free market economy:

> Beginning in the 1990s, getting a higher proportion of Americans to become homeowners became the political holy grail of government housing policies. ... They put pressure on the banks to lend to people who they would not otherwise lend to—namely, people with lower incomes, poorer credit ratings and little or no money for a conventional down payment of 20 percent of the price of a house. Such people were referred to politically as "the underserved population"—as if politicians know who should and who shouldn't get mortgages better than peo-

ple who have spent their careers making mortgage-lending decisions.[41]

Our constitutional form of government is based on individuals having equal natural rights. Our legal system is predicated upon one's standing in relation to the law—that is, plaintiff, respondent, government, and defendant. Nevertheless, for at least sixty years, group identity rather than the individual has become a reality in American politics. One group most often in the news is African-Americans. A bloody civil war was fought to obliterate obvious slavery. Nevertheless, more than a century later, American society still deals with the assumed guilt of the majority of the population. African-Americans are treated as victims who are entitled as beneficiaries of many government programs. Here are just two comments on that reality by Stein and Williams:

> Yet blacks, who have experienced the most thorough revolution in human advancement in world history over the past 50 years, are told by their would-be leaders that it's as if nothing has been accomplished—they're still living back in the days of the Klan. This is false, divisive, and extremely harmful. Unfortunately, there's no political capital to be made by the Left in acknowledging how good things are—their only advantage lies in claiming the White Citizen's Council and the Republican party are essentially identical. This is an *Alice in Wonderland* inversion of reality. It is also thoroughly cynical.[42]

> Intellectuals and political hustlers who blame the plight of so many blacks on poverty, discrimination and the "legacy of slavery" are complicit in the socioeconomic and moral decay. But as Booker T. Washington suggested, "There's another class of colored people who make a business of keeping the troubles, the wrongs, and the hardships of the Negro race before the public. Having learned that they are

able to make a living out of their troubles, they have grown into the settled habit of advertising their wrongs—partly because they want sympathy and partly because it pays. Some of these people do not want the Negro to lose his grievances, because they do not want to lose their jobs."[43]

All these government programs that provide employment, monetary payments, and preferential treatment constitute a powerful element within American society to preserve the status quo without giving thought to the reality that we are broke and we can no longer afford to continue doing business as usual. This was summarized in this concise statement: "There is a 'Taking Coalition' comprised of trial lawyers, public sector labor unions, big-city political machines, contractors, Nanny State radicals, and lots of folks who benefit from government handouts. The good guys, the 'Leave us Alone Coalition' believe in what our founding fathers believed; don't want other people's money; don't want other people taking our money. We want to start in business without being overtaxed and over regulated. We want to educate our kids where and how we see fit. [44]

In this chapter, the impact of the 16th Amendment fundamentally altered the power of the federal government with a constant flow of income tax revenue. The many acts of the New Deal, particularly passage of Social Security, altered the ability of individuals to claim freedom from federal encroachment on their property. The subsequent acts of the Great Society further solidified the gains of the progressive/statist agenda. With an increasing number of college graduates, and an increasing number of federal government programs, job opportunities and careers as politicians and bureaucrats became ever more attractive. This gave rise to the new aristocracy – the Cognoscenti – that will be covered in the next chapter.

3. The Cognoscenti: a new aristocracy and academic indoctrination

A new aristocracy - the Cognoscenti - perpetuates itself and is highly compensated. Many Cognoscenti come from academia that embraces the progressivism/statist agenda. In the classrooms, indoctrination erodes understanding of natural rights and limited government. Many graduates become teachers, professors, journalists, lawyers and judges perpetuating the progressive/statist agenda.

The Cognoscenti Perpetuates Itself and Is Highly Compensated

There is now a *de facto* new aristocracy that has emerged within American society comprising the governing class of elected politicians and high level appointed bureaucrats: the Cognoscenti. It would be helpful if scholars and journalists could agree upon using *the Cognoscenti* as one name, one nomenclature, to indicate clearly what others may call the ruling class or the government elite. It would be helpful if journalists and others who report or provide commentary on politics and government in America could settle on one term so everyone would know immediately who is being described and what platform they advocate. As explained in the preface of this book, *the Cognoscenti* refers to a governing class of those who think they know better than the rest of us. They are convinced government is and should be the solution to all social problems, and they are comprised of those politicians and government bureaucrats who subscribe to the progressive/statist agenda. That agenda is also synonymous with what others may call *modern liberalism, the left, left wing,* and *leftist* For Judge Robert Bork, these advocates of modern liberalism include "most of the Democratic Congressional party, some of the Republican Congressional party, and large sections of the judiciary, including, all too often, a majority of the U. S. Supreme Court."[1]

A problem of "brilliant elites" is that when men are most sure and most arrogant they are, quite often, most mistaken. Thomas Sowell points to the failures of wonderful ideas in government:

> Many of the wonderful-sounding ideas that have been tried as government policies have failed disastrously. One of the ideas that has proved to be almost impervious to evidence is the idea that wise and far-sighted people need to take control and plan economic and social policies so that there will be a rational and just order, rather than chaos resulting from things being allowed to take their own course. … It was the "brain trust" advisers whose policies are now increasingly recognized as having prolonged the Great Depression of the 1930s, while claiming credit for ending it. … Brainy folks were also present in Lyndon Johnson's administration where brilliant "whiz kids" tried to micro-manage the Vietnam War, with disastrous results. For creating a truly monumental disaster, you need people with high IQs. Such people have been told all their lives how brilliant they are. But they tend to over-estimate how important brilliance itself is when dealing with real-world problems.[2]

The best and the brightest often do not know their limitations and keep trying to do what the market might have done better without their help—or at least with more humble, cautious, restrained help.

The spirit of "all for one, one for all" was shared by all of FDR's Brain Trust, and they inherited it wholesale from Herbert Croly and his comrades. This has been the liberal enterprise ever since: to transform a democratic republic into an enormous tribal community, to give every member of society that sense of belonging that we allegedly feel in a close-knit community. [3]

Ben Stein and coauthor Phil DeMuth wrote *Can America Survive? The Rage of the Left, the Truth, and What to Do about It.* In this work they provide an original insight that the New Testament idea of "Phariseeism" motivates the elite in America, including many members of the Cognoscenti. Drawing upon personal experience and knowledge of the scriptures, they conclude that the feeling of being better than the rest of us is an age-old disease:

> Phariseeism is the belief that a man or woman can lay claim to moral superiority by certain austere habits of behavior, plain dress, and frugal living. ... The Pharisees were particularly called to account by Jesus Christ for their extreme sanctimony, and the certainty that they were better than others.... Phariseeism is an incredibly potent psychological tool because it transforms the inability of the Pharisee to get rich into a moral virtue. In its power to turn weakness into strength and strength into weakness, it's easy to see why Phariseeism is so appealing, especially to individuals in havens of fear and insecurity such as university towns. On a large scale, when an entire society is tarred with the brush of immorality for its supposed wastefulness. ... This attitude—that it is moral to criticize and belittle those who have more than we do—is dangerous. This kind of Pharisaical hatred of the U. S. because of our wealth creates a destructive climate of self-loathing and self-doubt, which robs us of the moral

confidence we need for the ongoing war against a super-Pharisaical terrorist class in the Islamic nations.[4]

The Cognoscenti see themselves as the best, so they function as a new aristocracy. The Free Online dictionary definition of aristocracy: "government by the best individuals or a small privileged class; a government in which power is vested in a minority consisting of those believed to be the best qualified." This new aristocracy perpetuates itself by hiring like-minded individuals.

Malcolm Gladwell wrote *The Tipping Point* that became a national best seller. Within this book, he discusses Dunbar's rule of 150, which describes the limits on the number of people with whom one can have truly meaningful relationships:

> Dunbar has actually developed an equation, which works for most primates, in which he plugs in what he calls the neocortex ratio of a particular species—the size of the neocortex relative to the size of the brain—and the equation spits out the expected maximum group size of the animal. If you plug in the neocortex ratio for Homo sapiens, you get a group estimate of 147.8—or roughly 150. "The figure 150 seems to represent the maximum number of individuals with whom we can have a genuinely social relationship, the kind of relationship that goes with knowing who they are and how they relate to us. Putting it another way, it's the number of people you would not feel embarrassed about joining uninvited for a drink if you happened to bump into them in a bar."... The Rule of 150 says that congregants in a rapidly expanding church, or the members of a social club, or anyone in a group activity banking on the epidemic spread of shared ideals needs to be particularly cognizant of the perils of bigness. Crossing the 150 line is a small change that can make a big difference.[5]

Evidence suggests current income inequality—which has grown to levels not seen since the Gilded Age—contributes to a self-selection of enrollment in elite universities, completion of graduate degrees, and then election to office or appointment to high-level bureaucratic positions. Here are two excerpts from the British newspaper *The Economist:*

> In 1980-2002 the share of total income earned by the top
> 0.1% of earners more than doubled. Intergenerational mo-
> bility may well be decreasing. The reason for this lies in the
> paradox at the heart of the new meritocracy. The gap in
> income between the college-educated and the non-college
> educated rose from 31% in 1979 to 66% in 1997. But
> social class increasingly determines access to college. The
> proportion of students from upper-income families at the
> country's elite colleges is growing once again. Only 3% of
> students in the most selective universities come from the
> bottom income quartile, and only 10% come from the
> bottom half of the income scale. The educated classes still
> do such a superb job of consolidating and transmitting
> their privileges.[6]

> For Americans, high social inequality is balanced by equal-
> ity of opportunity. The opportunity to get to the top
> pinnacles of financial and social success is enhanced by
> America's college system; especially, the big three universi-
> ties (Harvard, Yale and Princeton) that have for centuries
> created and reproduced the national elite. The Ivy League
> universities have defined and redefined merit according to
> their shifting institutional priorities.… Those who are able
> to define merit will almost invariably possess more of it,
> and those with greater resources—cultural, economic, and
> social—will generally be able to ensure that the educational
> system will deem their children more meritorious.[7]

This new aristocracy rewards itself with better-than-average compensation, benefits, and pensions provided by taxpayers. At the federal government level, many of the programs require regulation of or provide money and support to the business and professional-services segments of the economy. Consequently a higher proportion of the positions are filled with college graduates compared to the economy as a whole. "An alarming study by the libertarian Cato Institute suggests that a new class is being created in America—a government working elite with special privileges, quickly outpacing the private sector in the salaries and benefits it receives."[8]

Dick Morris shared his observations on how the Cognoscenti take advantage of the high compensation and other perquisites that are now available:

> Our modern plantation owners—people with unimaginable wealth—have no qualms in using the money of the middle class to buy the votes of the poor and do not worry about how these very taxes will block the middle classes' upward mobility. They kow-tow to public employee unions and let them destroy our government services in return for their votes and political support. They do not worry about bad public schools. With their own security guards, they don't care much about the quality of policing. When you're flying in private jets and being driven around in limos, why worry about public transportation? The rich men and women who have now become our senators, congressmen, governors, cabinet officers, and presidents use the power their money has bought them to buy off the masses with programs, and to enfeeble the upper middle class with taxes. They resort to the ultimate tax—inflation—to rob the wage-and salary-earners of the fruits of their enterprise. It is only through manipulating the power of government by acquiring political clout that one can advance.[9]

Here are two examples of the relatively better paying government positions published in California in the *Orange County Register*:

> There are similar staffing situations at the state and local levels of government. However, the local level has a high percentage of police and fire positions, and these are well paid primarily because of the inherent risk compared to other civilian positions. Overall the relative compensation for federal employees, including salary and benefits, was $123,049 in 2009 while private-sector workers made $61,051.[10]

> At the same time, the federal workforce became the largest ever in this nation's history at 2.15 million. And that did not include nearly 650,000 postal workers or the number of employees who worked for firms under contract to government agencies. More amazing, "during this recession, the percentage of federal workers earning $100,000 or more a year has exploded from 14 percent to 19 percent. Nearly one in five federal workers now earn six-figure salaries, before bonuses and overtime."[11]

These are examples that are catching the attention of the general public that public servants are being compensated at a far greater level than what they received during the *Manifest Destiny* period (1789-1912). During the formative years of this nation, citizens paid more attention to what was going on with their local government. Many took part in serving in public office part-time while still working at their normal occupations. Now, when citizens fail to pay attention, outrageous salary and benefit levels can result. Most egregiously, in Orange County, California, my home county, "a city manager was making $787,637 per year; the police chief was making $457,000 per year; and the part-time city council members voted themselves roughly $100,000 annually."[12] Another example of the public not paying attention occurred at the state level in California. Dozens of former employees of Governor Arnold Schwarzenegger were reassigned to other jobs and board member positions, and at least half went to higher-paying positions:

> Eleven former staffers were given jobs with state salaries of more than $100,000 a year. Just a few of those appointed saw their salaries decrease. In 2004, Schwarzenegger vowed to get rid of 88 boards and commissions, including the Integrated Waste Management Board (IWMB) and Unemployment Insurance Appeals Board (UIAB). "No one paid by the state should make $100,000 for only meeting twice a month," he said. Now, two of his former aides were appointed to $117,818 and $113,191 positions on the IWMB and another aid was appointed to the UIAB for $114,191, giving her a raise of $9,191 a year.[13]

The general public is now more aware of the extent to which public employee labor unions contribute to the Democratic Party in exchange for favorable treatment when it comes time to collectively bargain for wages, hours, and other working conditions. As one example, columnist Daniel Weintraub reported on the public engineers union that contributed $200,000 to reelect California governor Gray Davis in 2002 and then nearly $400,000 a year later when Davis was facing a recall election. Davis lost.[14]

The topic of pensions for government workers has gradually come to light as a huge weight on the economy and the well being of future generations. When the unfounded liabilities of federal, state, and municipal pensions are added together, it amounts to a staggering $100 trillion—and just when the federal deficit is more than $15 trillion, the equivalent of the entire gross domestic product for one year. Ian Murray has written a well-researched book identifying the many ways that the government fat cats (the Cognoscenti) take advantage of their positions of power and control. His title is self-explanatory: *Stealing You Blind: How Government Fat Cats are Getting Rich Off of You.* He makes this observation:

We need to overhaul how federal workers are paid: automatic pay raises need to go, as do seniority-based pay scales, and the virtual immunity of federal workers from being fired. Working for the federal government should not be a way to get gold-plated benefits and a salary you couldn't match in the private sector. We need to get back to the idea of "public service," where government workers—on the public payroll—don't make more than taxpayers in comparable jobs. Unaffordable government pension schemes (should be replaced with) a 403(b) plan—the non-profit version of the 401(k).[15]

Many within Academia Embrace the Progressive/Statist Agenda

Academia refers to higher education, university and college level, and the scholars who teach and do research in that environment. In a more general sense, it refers to the cultural accumulation of knowledge and its transmission across the generations. As recently as 1940, only 5 percent of Americans were college graduates. However, one consequence of World War II was to provide the GI Bill to millions of veterans, and they used those monies to obtain college educations. The idea of a college degree as a means to a more affluent career took hold among their children, grandchildren, and great-grandchildren. As a result, today there are at least 25 percent of the population holding a bachelor's or graduate-level degree. This greatly expanded availability of college graduates provides a recruitment pool for those aspiring to careers as part of the Cognoscenti.

The ideas of progressivism and statism took root within academia, and they are with us to this day. Bork wrote a warning about this unnoticed change in the intellectual climate:

This time we face an attack. …The enemy within is *modern liberalism*, a corrosive agent carrying a very different mood and agenda than that of classical or traditional liberalism. "Modern Liberalism" may not be quite the correct name for what I have in mind…. If you do not think "modern liberalism" an appropriate name, substitute "radical liberalism" or "sentimental liberalism" or even, save us, "postmodern liberalism."[16]

Those in the cultural elite are called by different names: the intelligentsia, the intellectual elite, public intellectuals, the clerisy, the professorate, and the academic elite. The intelligentsia can be described as a social class of people engaged in complex mental and creative labor directed toward the development and dissemination of culture, encompassing intellectuals and social groups close to them (e.g., artists and school teachers). According to the Free Online dictionary, the term *intelligentsia* is defined as the educated or intellectual people in a society or community. Bork draws insights regarding Joseph Schumpeter's intellectuals that may explain both their hostility and their fantasizing:

> Intellectuals are in fact people who wield the power of the spoken and the written word, and one of the touches that distinguish them from other people who do the same is the absence of direct responsibility for practical affairs. … Intellectuals are an important cultural force nonetheless. Because they wield the power of language and symbols, their values and ideas are broadcast by the press, movies, television, universities, primary and secondary schools, books and magazines, philanthropies, foundations, and many churches. Thus, intellectuals are influential out of all proportion to their numbers.[17]

A significant number in the academic world may fall into the trap of falling for an ideology, according to Daniel J. Flynn, author of *Intellectual Morons*.

> For the true believer, ideology (provides) stock answers, conditioned responses, and delivers one-size fits all expla-

nations for complex political and cultural questions. When intellectuals let ideology do their thinking, we can't with any justification continue to label them intellectuals. ... But dangers arise when the perceived morality of the mission allows immorality—lying for the cause, forcing the "good" upon society, self-righteousness, etc. to corrupt the crusaders. ... It is intentions rather than outcomes that matter for such people.[18]

Flynn observes how intellectuals become so arrogant and come to the conclusion they are better than the rest of us:

Ideologues are prone to mistaking their ideal for the real. ... From an early age, smart people are reminded of their intelligence; intellectuals tend to have an inflated sense of their own wisdom; arrogance, not intelligence, leads them into trouble; hubris compels them to believe that they can run everyone else's life.[19]

Flynn describes Herbert Marcuse as an example of what it means for an intellectual to be a statist:

In the academic world, it means that you embrace the ideas of Herbert Marcuse, who was the pop philosopher of the New Left. He urged his fellow academics to oppose freedom of speech within academe, for such freedom produced too many criticisms of communism. All opponents of socialism were to be denied free speech in Marcuse's ideal world. There is no need for logic, debate, and the free exchange of ideas, said Marcuse, for Marxism provides all the "correct" answers. Following Marcuse, the politically correct statists within academe believe that the totalitarian societies of the world represent "freedom" and that people "must be forced to be free," i.e., to acquiesce in socialism.[20]

The influence of Marxism also permeates many classroom presentations. A widely held Marxist view is that intellectuals are alienated and anti-establishment. Although Marx seemed to imply in his reference to intellectuals that they are constantly engaged in an instinctive struggle with established institutions, including the state, such a struggle could be carried on within such institutions and in support of established institutions and against change. Ben Stein has commented on how Marxists interest themselves in the status of intellectuals for a number of reasons.

> The reason socialism, or something like it, will never die is because the socialist ideology satisfies some of our most potent psychological needs: power, control, significance in life, and so on. Karl Marx said "All history is the history of class struggle." It was a beguiling hypothesis, but it's since fallen flat on its face. Working people don't want to annihilate the middle class; instead, they want to be a *part* of the middle class and then the upper class—and many do just that in America. Class analysis of history has proved useful, however, as a means of providing well-paid work and power to intellectuals, who are the best and most brutal at class analysis. This covers up otherwise bizarre usurpations of authority by people who want to control their fellow human beings. It's natural and normal, and we assume all people do it—that is, use moral principles to rationalize their own desires and wishes....Socialism serves the psychological needs of certain human beings, just as political orders built on the blueprints of Jefferson and Madison appeal to those of us who like freedom.[21]

Stein points out how this Marxist outlook does not correspond to the reality of America as he has come to know and understand it:

> One can look at the Left's analysis of America. ... Is the problem economic exploitation? Is America really a society

of a few wealthy users riding on the backs of a vast army of serf like laborers? Hardly.... You'd never know it to hear the leftists in this country talk. ... By all historical measurements, America is a tolerant, open, welcoming, nurturing society that has generally acted in a magnanimous and beneficent way to the world at large and most especially to its own people.[22]

Within academia professors hire and promote people with whom they are most comfortable—people who share their progressive/statist agenda. The reality of academia is that it is a community in itself, distinct in its mission, values, and structure from the larger society. In accordance with the rule of 150, informal group norms determine who is in and who is not. Here are two examples written by George F. Will and Thomas Potase:

A filtering process, from graduate school admissions through tenure decisions, tends to exclude conservatives from academia's "sheltered habitat." The "first protocol" requires that in order to enter the profession, your work must be deemed, by the criteria of the prevailing culture, "relevant." This gives rise to the "false consensus effect," which occurs when, due to institutional provincialism, people think that the collective opiniOn of their own group matches that of the larger population....When like-minded people deliberate as an organized group, the general opinion shifts toward extreme versions of their common beliefs. They become tone deaf to the way they sound to others outside their closed circle of belief. Many campuses are intellectual versions of one-party nations. US campuses have more insistently proclaimed their commitment to diversity. They do indeed cultivate diversity—in race, skin color, ethnicity, and sexual preference. In everything but thought.[23]

After a 30-year career as a university professor, I was one of the six conservatives out of the 250 faculty members at my small California university. ... I have sat on many hiring committees. The first goal in candidate selection is to be sure the candidate will fit in and support the other professors. Since the liberal professors (the majority) do the hiring, they will almost always hire people with their same liberal views—the people they are comfortable with. In the intensely competitive struggle to gain promotion and tenure within the university system, social conformity is a must. Existing faculty members as a group must specifically approve any promotion and the decision to grant tenure. Thus, fitting in, getting along, having very good human relations with other faculty members and strongly supporting group norms [the progressive/socialist agenda] are absolute musts. Within liberal institutions, conservative ideas are attacked. The students are presented with only one view of the world that they must (at least temporarily) support to pass the course with a good grade.[24]

Indoctrination Erodes Understanding of Natural Rights and Limited Government

In a 2008 essay, Herb Meyers describes his view of what is wrong with contemporary American public education and the extent to which indoctrination is occurring. Instead of calling it indoctrination, Meyers describes it as "the implanting of political prisms in the minds of the youth."

Let me put this as starkly as I can: What's going on today is a kind of domestic Cold War—a seemingly endless standoff, with the occasional hard skirmish—between those of us who see the US for what it really is, and those who are seeing the US through a prism. No one is born with a political prism in his or her mind. It has to be implanted there. And for more than 40 years, since the mid-1960s, this is what the Left [progressive/statists] has been working to do. They have been working—steadily and stealthily—to implant political prisms into the minds of Americans. They've done this by seizing control of our public education system, and of our mainstream media. Today, our schools and universities are less designed to educate our children than they are designed to indoctrinate them into believing that the United States is an evil country in which the rich oppress the poor, in which business pollutes rather than produces, and whose armed forces wreak havoc around the world rather than keep us safe while liberating entire populations from tyranny. And the mainstream media is less focused on informing than on reinforcing what our schools and universities are teaching.

Forty years of hard work by the Left [progressive/statists] have paid off. Our schools, our universities, and the mainstream media have successfully implanted political prisms into the minds of nearly half our population. That's why so many of our elections are so close, why so many key Supreme Court cases are decided by five-to-four votes, and why we always seem to be split down the middle on whatever issue confronts us—the war, the economy, immigration, healthcare, energy, the environment, and all the rest.[25]

Many Graduates Perpetuate the Progressive/Statist Agenda

College and university classrooms, especially within the humanities, social sciences, and interdisciplinary studies, are being used to put forth only one accepted ideology (progressive/statist agenda) that indoctrinates new batches of recruits every year while marginalizing other points of view (i.e. constitutional conservatism). "The academy (is) the boot camp and parade ground of the contemporary Left."[26] Walter Williams made this observation of how ridiculous it is for parents to pay outlandish college tuitions in order to expose their children to anti-Americanism and other academic nonsense occurring because of academic indoctrination:

> Many professors, mostly on the liberal side of the political spectrum, use their classrooms to proselytize students. ... While acceptable at most universities, it is nothing less than academic dishonesty to do so. ... Learning how to think straight, as opposed to what values and opinions to hold, is the crucial part of education. ... Parents are paying an average tuition of $21,000, and at some colleges over $40,000 to have their children exposed to anti-Americanism and academic nonsense.[27]

Why in the heck are we spending taxpayer dollars to fund these ongoing efforts at indoctrination and proselytizing? Here is an important consideration raised by George Will.

> Schools of Social Work mandate an ideological orthodoxy to which students must subscribe concerning "social justice" and "oppression."... In 1997, the political agenda declares that promoting "social and economic justice" is especially imperative as a response to "the conservative trends of the past three decades."... Because many schools of social work proclaim "conservatives need not apply," two questions arise: Why are such schools of indoctrination permitted in institutions of higher education? And why are people of all political persuasions taxed to finance this propaganda?[28]

Two related groups that may fall prey to ideology are journalists and Hollywood writers. Journalists tend to pursue questions that interest them. When the press corps is more than 80 percent Democratic, their stories tend to reflect Democrat's interests. To some extent this is a problem of self-selection. Journalism attracts people who want to right wrongs, and the generation running journalism schools and media businesses came of age when government, especially the federal government, was seen as the solution to most wrongs. These executives, like the tenured radicals in law schools and the rest of academia, hired ideological cronies and shaped their institutions to reflect their views. They keep meticulous tabs on the race and gender and ethnic backgrounds of their students and faculty. Stein used his experiences in Washington and Hollywood to add these observations about Americans' assault against America:

> In a word, there's a sustained assault against America, by Americans.... There is a dismaying crypto-civil war that's being fought in the classrooms, on TV screens, and in our legislature. (It is being waged by) men and women paid for by inheritances, foundation grants, the astronomical salaries of Hollywood, and the U. S Congress.[29]

> Hollywood writers are a disproportionately, ideologically powerful group because they're the "intellectuals" of the town. ... Hollywood scribes ... feel envious of the business people they meet. ... Marxism—as a basic, easy-to-grasp way of pretending to be moral while wielding a big, gold-plated stick—attached itself like a leech to Hollywood in the 1930s and really never let go. It became the lay religion of the town, the groupthink in certain (but by no means all) Hollywood inside circles. ... Alas, the most angry and anti-American of the powers in Hollywood gets most of the ink—the quiet, hardworking people are, well, quiet.[30]

Progressive influence on law-school faculty and graduates contributes to membership in the Cognoscenti. A study of voter registration among law-school faculty affirms the dominance of one point of view—the progressive/statist agenda:

The left has a lock on law schools. Democrats outnumber Republicans by 8 to 1 at the law schools. Some academics argue that their political ideologies don't affect the way they teach, which proves how detached they've become from reality in their monocultures. The claim is especially dubious if you're training lawyers to deal with controversial public policies. ... But the lack of political diversity is taken as a matter of course. As long as the professors look different, why worry if they all think the same?[31]

Thomas Sowell makes these observations about how the progressive/statist agenda impacts those who are selected to serve as judges. It is worth emphasizing the outlook of the progressive/statists that it is desirable to have the law in the hands of "a progressive and enlightened caste." This describes how the new aristocracy see themslves:

Professor Roscoe Pound likewise referred to the need for "a living constitution by judicial interpretation," in order to "respond to the vital needs of present-day life." He rejected the idea of law as "a body of rules." But if law is not a body of rules, what is it? A set of arbitrary fiats by judges, imposing their own vision of "the needs of the times"? Or a set of arbitrary regulations stealthily emerging from within the bowels of a bureaucracy? As Roscoe Pound put it, law should be *"in the hands of a progressive and enlightened caste whose conceptions are in advance of the public* (italics added)." That is still the vision of the left a hundred years later. Louis Brandeis cited "newly arisen social needs" and "a shifting of our longing from legal justice to social justice." In other words, judges were encouraged to do an end run around rules, such as those set forth in the Constitution, and around the elected representatives of "we the people."[32]

Judge Bork wrote *The Tempting of America: The Political Seduction of the Law* to call attention to a significant problem within the American judicial system. Over-simplifying, he charges that political considerations are taking precedence over true jurisprudence. In his book, he makes clear why it's important to understand how the progressive/statist agenda has permeated law schools and the legal profession:

> Judges are by definition members of the intellectual class and, in addition, for professional and personal reasons, tend to be influenced by the culture of the law schools. Like most people, judges tend to accept the assumptions of the culture that surrounds them, often without fully understanding the foundations of those assumptions or their implications.[33]

> [Faculty adhering to the progressive/statist agenda] have overrun a number of law schools, including a large majority of America's most prestigious, where the lawyers and judges of the future are being trained. ... But the focus of the struggle ... is control of the courts and the Constitution. ... Why? Because the Constitution is the trump card in American politics, and judges decide what the Constitution means.[34]

That point about "deciding what the Constitution means" is critical to understanding the danger that looms ahead. In recent years, the process of confirming justices by the US Senate has become very contentious. Bork's nomination resulted in a new word to describe unfavorable treatment by the Senate: "Borking." Columnist Morton Kondracke remarked that the "judicial confirmation system has come to resemble nothing less than gag warfare, making the chances of dignified proceedings slim, even in wartime."[35]

In this chapter, there was an explanation of a new aristocracy - the Cognoscenti – that perpetuates itself and is highly compensated. Within academia, many embrace the progressivism/statist agenda. In the classrooms, indoctrination erodes understanding of natural rights and limited government. Many of these same graduates go on to become teachers, professors, journalists, lawyers and judges perpetuating the progressive/statist agenda. In the next chapter 4, one of the contributors to future danger to America is the presidency. This relates to an often-overlooked fact that the president nominates members of the Supreme Court and the federal appellate courts. When a majority that adhere to the progressive/statist agenda dominates these judicial positions, the forthcoming outcomes could quickly transform America into something quite opposite of what the Founding Fathers created.

4. Tipping into majority tyranny and soft despotism

For nearly 5,000 years of recorded history, tyranny as some variation of the "divine right of kings" prevailed until 1689. In addition, the Founding Fathers were educated to understand that pure democracy can lead to either oligarchy or majority tyranny. After establishing a representative democracy, Alexis de Tocqueville gave warnings about the future danger from soft despotism. Given the prevailing economic, social and demographic realities, the Democratic Party has the potential of becoming the nucleus of a majority tyranny. Also, as a demagogue, President Obama has the potential to transform America into a perpetual soft despotism.

The Divine Right of Kings

Believing in the "divine right of kings," tyranny prevailed for thousands of years until it was curtailed in England in 1689. *Tyranny* and *majority tyranny* are examples of terms Americans use without appreciating their full meaning. The online dictionary Wicktionary defines them this way:

> *Tyranny:* A government in which a single ruler (a tyrant) has absolute power. The office or jurisdiction of an absolute ruler. Absolute power, or its use. Extreme severity or rigour.
> *Majority tyranny*: A situation in which a government or other authority democratically supported by a majority of its subjects

        makes policies or takes actions benefiting that majority, with-
out regard for the rights or welfare of the rest of its subjects.

How does tyranny happen? To answer that question, let's consider that
recorded history is only about six thousand years old, during which time
there have been plenty of examples of tyranny. Prior to recorded history,
during the prehistoric eons, mankind survived by hunting, fishing, and
gathering fruits, nuts, and other edible matter. Early man most likely survived by living in small groups called *bands*. Members of a band were family or close relatives, so there was no need for any formal government.

After the discovery of agriculture, roughly ten thousand years ago, mankind started living in a more settled fashion by establishing villages, then small
cities.[1] As populations increased bands formed into the next level of organization—what we now call *tribes*. Most likely, tribes functioned without formal
structure because most members were still related by blood or marriage. Conflict situations usually could be resolved by informal means.[2]

As tribes grew larger, sometimes absorbing other tribes, the next level
of organization—the chiefdom—came into existence. The chief established
rules of behavior; resolved disputes among members; and soon the office
of chief became hereditary.[3] When chiefdoms overwhelmed or conquered
neighboring tribes or chiefdoms, the "super" chief became known as a *king*
and his realm was a *state* or *kingdom*. Now the potential for tyranny was
in place. When the kings perceived that they had "god-like" powers, they
concluded that they were indeed representatives of the gods on earth. Some
kings took the next step and declared that they *were* gods and were to be
worshipped. Members of the kingdoms became *subjects*.

When the kings declared that they ruled by "divine right," government
had unlimited power over individuals. For thousands of years thereafter,
men were subjects of tyrannical rule from monarchs, kings, emperors,
or despots. Of course there were still many places where tribes survived
separate from nearby kingdoms and empires. Within the kingdoms and
empires, the majority of people could exercise tyranny over any minority
living among them. For example the Jews were considered minorities in
Egypt, Assyria, and Babylon.

After the fall of the Roman Empire in 476 AD, a period of political and economic chaos descended on what is now known as Europe. Over many centuries, there was a constant threat of invasions by various peoples known as the Huns, Vandals, Moors, Vikings, Tatars, and Mongols. In response to this, the system of *feudalism* came into being. In order to have some protection, the common people came under the rule of armed knights who took on titles such as baron, duke, marquis, earl, or count. These noblemen lived in castles and maintained small armies of knights and men-at-arms. The common people, known as *serfs*, were in bond to the local lord. The term serf gives rise to the term serfdom that we will discuss at the end of chapter 9.

In the British Isles several centuries of internal warfare concluded in 1485, when Henry VII started the Tudor Dynasty. His son Henry VIII founded the Church of England. His daughter became Queen Elizabeth who had a long reign that ended in 1603. Her relative in Scotland became King James I of England, who believed fully in the "divine right of kings." A civil war erupted during the reign of his son, Charles I. The parliamentary forces under Oliver Cromwell defeated King Charles I, charged him with treason, and executed him—the first time this was ever done to a ruling monarch (1649). This effectively put an end to the notion of the "divine right of kings."

William and Mary became co-rulers of England (1688), and Parliament passed the *Bill of Rights* in 1689. At the same time, John Locke wrote *The Second Treatise on Government*, which included arguments for the natural rights to life, liberty, and property and the people's duty to revolt against unjust government. Both of these documents were influential in the formulation of the American Declaration of Independence and the Federal Constitution.

Pure Democracy Can Lead to Majority Tyranny

The Founding Fathers concluded that pure democracy does not work over time, because it can lead to either oligarchy or majority tyranny.

Democracy is another term Americans use without appreciating its full meaning. The online Oxford dictionary defines it this way:

> *Democracy:* a system of government by the whole population or all the eligible members of a state, typically through elected representatives.

John Adams wrote and published *A Defence of the Constitutions of Government of the United States of America* in three volumes in 1787. He compiled descriptions of modern and ancient governments. Adams concluded that the leadership of a democracy would always come from what he called the "aristocratical" class:

> Congress will always be composed of members from the natural and artificial aristocratical body in every state, even in the northern, as well as in the middle and southern states. Their natural dispositions then, in general, will be (whether they shall be sensible of it or not, and whatever integrity or abilities they may be possessed of) to diminish the prerogatives of the governors, and the privileges of the people, and to augment the influence of the aristocratical parties.[4]

In the *Federalist Papers*, Madison, Hamilton, and Jay argued for ratification of the Constitution, asserting that throughout history pure democracy has led to tyranny. "The Founders envisioned a republican form of government, but as Benjamin Franklin warned, 'When the people find they can vote themselves money, that will herald the end of the republic.' "[5]

Warnings about the future Danger from Soft Despotism

Alexis de Tocqueville (1805-1859), a French nobleman, warned of the future danger of trading liberty for the soft despotism of government security. He visited the United States for two years when the population of the twenty-four existing states was around thirteen million. After returning to France, he published his major findings as *Democracy in America* (in two volumes in 1835 and 1840). Here are a few examples of de Tocqueville's reasoning, excerpted from book one:

> The very essence of democratic government consists in the absolute sovereignty of the majority; for there is nothing in democratic states that is capable of resisting it. Most of the American constitutions [he refers to the states as well as federal] have sought to increase this natural strength of the majority by artificial means. Of all political institutions, the legislature is the one that is most easily swayed by the will of the majority. The Americans determined that the people should elect the members of the legislature directly, and for a very brief term, in order to subject them, not only to the general convictions, but also even to the daily passions, of their constituents. … It is to a legislature thus constituted that almost all the authority of the government has been entrusted.[6]

> In my opinion, the main evil of the present democratic institutions of the United States does not arise, as is often asserted in Europe, from their weakness, but from their irresistible strength. I am not so much alarmed at the excessive liberty that reigns in that country as at the inadequate securities which one finds there against tyranny. When an individual or a party is wronged in the United States, to whom can he apply for redress? If to public opinion, public opinion constitutes the majority; if to the legislature, it represents the majority and implicitly obeys it; if to the executive power, it is appointed by the majority and serves as a passive tool in its hands. The public force consists of the majority under arms; the jury is the majority invested with the right of hearing judicial cases; and in certain states even the judges are elected by the majority. However iniquitous or

> absurd the measure of which you can complain, you must submit to it as well as you can.[7]

> I do not say that there is a frequent use of tyranny in America at the present day; but I maintain that there is no sure barrier against it, and that the causes which mitigate the government there are to be found in the circumstances and the manners of the country more than in its laws.[8]

Democracy left to itself tends to surrender liberty to the passion for security and equality, and thus to end in soft despotism—the hardest kind to stop and eradicate. When despotism comes with the smiling face of a gently scolding nanny, it's too easy to delude oneself into thinking little is to be gained by rebellion. The fear of losing small comforts keeps many a man glued to his couch. The fact is that the loss of liberty leads immediately to a loss of every other value. The material ones are the first and least important to go.

Despotism in the future has been painted starkly in two novels—*Nineteen-Eighty Four* by British socialist George Orwell and *Brave New World* by British pacifist Aldous Huxley. These are known as *dystopian* novels for they take the idea of a paradise—a utopia—and turn it into the opposite: a hell on earth. Orwell's work is set in the near future, and it describes despotism in terms of the Thought Police (who are everywhere), two-way televisions to monitor individual behavior, and "Newspeak," the government constructed language for everyday communication that inhibits abstract or creative thinking.

Huxley's work is set six hundred years after the death of Henry Ford. In that future world, there is no marriage; babies are cloned in laboratories and bred to fit into one of five categories. Alphas are the rulers and holders of the highest positions in society. Everyone is kept on a drug called soma in order to feel happy all the time. After age thirty, everyone is scheduled for a state-run end-of-life experience.

In a brilliant analysis of the underlying premise that leads to the progressive/statist agenda, Mark Levin focuses on utopianism, the attempt to bring an ideal world into present times:

In *Ameritopia*, I explain that the heart of the problem is, in fact, utopianism ... the ideological and doctrinal foundation for statism. . . . Utopianism has long promoted the idea of a paradisiacal existence and advanced concepts of pseudo "ideal" societies in which an heroic despot, a benevolent sovereign, or an enlightened oligarchy claims the ability and authority to provide for all the needs and fulfill all the wants of the individual—in exchange for his abject servitude.[9]

It's much easier to depict what soft despotism could look like under the increasing power and control of the Cognoscenti. Mark Steyn, who has a wonderful gift for writing, sees the following in our future:

As I say somewhere in my recent book, you don't need a president-for-life if you've got a bureaucracy-for-life. More and more aspects of the citizen's daily existence are regulated by rules and officials both of which are ever more disconnected from any meaningful accountability to the people's representatives. As the president says, look for even more "flexibility" in a second term: more non-recess recess appointments, more executive orders, and more bewildering innovation from the commissars of the hyper-regulatory state.[10]

The Democratic Party as the Nucleus of Majority Tyranny

With enough votes, the Democratic Party can potentially become the nucleus of a majority tyranny. Over many decades the Democratic Party evolved into a liberal labor party. Author Ben Stein does not lump all members of the Democratic Party under the same umbrella:

First of all, we don't think that all Democrats are miscreants, traitors, or fools. ... We don't see all the liberals in

government as evil people bent on national destruction. ...
Further, we don't see all liberal journalists as cranks and
saboteurs. ... We're troubled about the people who see
America as a late link in the unending chain of capitalist
(or male) oppression and seek ... to tear down and never to
enhance or improve.[11]

Prior to the Great Depression, all of American organized labor opposed
the extension of government power. In fact, the New Deal led to a huge
expansion in the federal government's power to tax, spend and regulate, including a Social Security system to help the aged and government agencies
to monitor the affairs of business.

The union membership exploded from a little more than
3 million in 1927 (11.3 percent of the non-agricultural
workforce) to more than 8 million in 1939 (28.6 percent of
the nonagricultural workforce). The unions also deepened
their relationship with the Democratic Party.[12]

The Democratic Party has moved to the radical Left ever since the
1960s. "Radical liberals won the war for the soul of the Democratic Party,
not least because of elaborate changes in the party's constitution that gave
minorities extra delegates. The Irish machine politicians, trade union boss-
es and Southern conservatives who had dominated the party for decades
began to lose out to antiwar protesters, feminists and environmentalists.
Reformism had mutated into radicalism, with something of an anti-Amer-
ican bent."[13]

Jonah Goldberg explains it this way: "The Sixties were born at the
AFL-CIO camp at Port Huron, Michigan in June, 1962. This was an
early convention of the SDS, a small group of alienated, left wing college
students. The Port Huron Statement was a well-intentioned declaration of
democratic optimism and admirable honesty. The authors conceded that
they were in fact bourgeois radicals, 'bred in at least modest comfort."[14]
Bork describes his view of how the Port Huron Statement provided the

kernel that led to elements of the New Left capturing the Democratic Party:

> The Port Huron Statement was the most widely circulated document of the New Left. Starting from a draft by Tom Hayden, the statement set forth the SDS agenda for changing human beings, the nation, and the world. ... They lacked specifics about how they would reform the world, what the end product would look like, and what was to be done if the world proved intractable.[15]

> One of the New Left's ambitions was to move the Democratic Party further to the left of the American center, to convert it to a more radical stance from the traditional liberal-labor ideology the party had espoused since FDR built his coalition. ... The formulations of the Sixties are now deeply embedded in our opinion-forming institutions and our culture. In the end, the spirit of Port Huron triumphed: it did change the world. Whether that change is permanent remains to be seen.[16]

> The idea that everything is ultimately political has taken hold. We know its current form as "political correctness," a distemper that afflicts the universities.[17]

David Horowitz has explained in an online essay that members of the New Left are adept at mobilizing public support, calling forth class warfare against the wealthy, and successfully making use of the tactics outlined by Saul Alinsky. The emergence of the Occupy Wall Street movement makes clear the difference in that the radicals are fighting a take-no-prisoners war; conservatives are not aware that they are in a war. The demonstrations seems consistent with the tactics as explained by Horowitz:

The first chapter of Alinsky's *Rules for Radicals* explains that "The life of man upon earth is a warfare." For Alinsky and his Machiavellian radicals, politics is war. ... Because radicals see politics as a war, they perceive opponents of their causes as enemies on a battlefield and set out to destroy them by demonizing and discrediting them personally. ... This is because when you are in a war—there is no middle ground. A war by definition is a fight to the finish. Enemies must be eliminated—either totally defeated or effectively destroyed. Conservatives don't really have such an enemy and therefore are not mentally in the war at all, which is why they often seem so defenseless or willing to throw their fellow conservatives over the side when they are attacked. ... Consequently, there is no real parallelism in this conflict. One side is fighting with a no-holds-barred, take-no-prisoners battle plan against the system, while the other is trying enforce its rules of fairness and pluralism (which of course does not mean that individual conservatives never break them).[18]

Two somewhat overlapping groups—the Latino population and the non-taxpaying population—potentially can move the Democratic Party into becoming a majority tyranny Among minority groups in America, more than 90 percent of African-Americans vote for Democratic candidates. The Hispanic population, which is much larger and more diverse, also votes mostly for Democrats. Because of differing birth rates, the non-Hispanic white population is decreasing as a percentage of the total population:

Five years ago, the AP reported whites are now in the minority in nearly one in 10 U.S. counties. Fueled by immigration and higher birth rates among blacks and Hispanics, there is a straining of race relations and sparking of a backlash against immigrants in many communities. Out of 58 counties in California, in 20 of the counties the non-Hispanic whites were in the minority, with the five lowest showing these percentages: Imperial (17.3), Los Angeles (29.2), Monterey (36.3), Fresno (36.4) and San Bernardino (37.2).[19]

Under current federal tax policy, roughly 44 percent of the American population pays no federal income tax. David Dickey wrote an op-ed piece putting this in perspective:

> Those who look to government as the solution to abuses of power are calling for the fox to guard the henhouse. It is always in government's self-interest to grow itself and thereby continually extend its power base. ... Unfortunately, with half of U.S. households receiving government payments of some sort, it is a rare candidate indeed that would propose such radical actions (reducing entitlement programs). Equally rare are voters who would support such a candidate, fearing that it might result in a reduction of their particular government payment or business support.[20]

Thus, with a majority of ethnic minority groups voting Democrat, and with a rough majority of the total voting population likely to vote Democrat in order to preserve the "goodies" they now receive from the government, we can conclude that the Democratic Party has the potential to become a permanent majority party.

As a Demagogue, Obama can Seduce America into Perpetual Soft Despotism

For progressives in the nineteenth century, the underlying premise of the State as the focus of politics created a desire for the familiarity of having a single leader, the prevailing form of government that had been in place for thousands of years. The founding fathers purposely constructed a government to protect individual liberty from the normal pattern of tyranny. This meant not allowing too much power in any of the three branches of government. This made no sense to the progressives, because government as a whole could not be held accountable to the people's will without a single accountable leader. Folsom explains further:

> Woodrow Wilson—both as a Ph.D. in history and as a two-term president—represented a break with the Constitution and its constrained view of history. Government, in Wilson's progressive view, did not exist merely to protect rights. The limited government enshrined in both the Declaration and the Constitution may have been an advance for the Founders, Wilson conceded, but society had evolved since then. Separation of powers was inefficient and hindered modern government from promoting progress. A strong executive was needed, Wilson believed, to translate the interest of the people into public policy. The president was the opinion leader, the "spokesman for the real sentiment and purpose of the country." And what the country needed was "a man who will be and who will seem to the country in some sort of embodiment of the character and purpose it wishes its government to have—a man who understood his own day and the needs of his country."[21]

In 1890 Wilson wrote about the true leader: "He must not traffic in subtleties and nuance, as literary men do. Rather, he must speak to stir their passions, not their intellects. *In short, he must be a skillful demagogue*(italics added for emphasis)."[22] Ronald Prestitto and William Atto elaborate on three aspects of the president as taking on the mantle of being the national leader:

> For the national political institutions to be genuinely democratic, Wilson contended, there had to be an identifiable leader, to whom the public could make known its will and whom it could hold elect orally accountable for success of failure in implementing that will throughout the whole of government. Wilson called upon the president to tran-

scend the separation of powers—to consider himself not merely as chief of a single branch of government, but as the popular leader of the whole of national politics. Wilson argued for the "political" function of the president, where he could use his connection to public opinion as a tool for moving all of the branches of government in the direction called for by the people. In this way Wilson believed the separation of powers system could be circumvented, and the enhanced presidency could be a means of energizing the kind of active national government that the progressive agenda required. These attitudes did not correspond to reality.

First of all, the Founding Fathers never intended to have a pure democracy, such as John Adams described in ancient Athens and Carthage, or in more modern Switzerland or Biscay.

Second, the Founding Fathers made clear that they had no intention of having one branch more accountable to the people than the other two.

Third, the president was viewed as having charge over foreign and military affairs. From the founders' perspective, the most dangerous aspect of Wilson's vision for the presidency would have been that the president's power was to come directly from the people as opposed to the Constitution. Wilson envisioned a president who would move the institutions of national government by the force of that popularity.... Wilson viewed the president as the national leader and originator of the national political agenda. [23]

Moving up to the present day, President Barack Obama, who, though lacking obvious qualifications, was elected to bring about "hope and change." Angelo Codevilla reviews six books to provide more insight into what Obama has actually been doing over the years compared to what he said during his election campaign:

In our time, how did a young man of scarce achievement get into position to win the Democratic Party's nomination for president? Because fully to know where anyone is going requires grasping whence he comes, let us open ourselves to wonder how, minus miracles, a 10-year-old boy without obvious talent who had lived in Indonesia since age six

ends up with an eight-year scholarship to Hawaii's most exclusive school;

a scholarship to Occidental College;

a transfer into Columbia University;

acceptance into Harvard Law School, and editorship of its law review; and

how he goes from job to prestigious job without apparently mastering any of the previous ones. No wonder some of Barack Obama's supporters treat him as if he were anointed by an extraterrestrial power.

Intellectually, Obama has always been a consumer, having left no record of formulating new ideas or of penetrating old ones. Politically, he is a follower and figurehead: having grown up in the ever branching stream of socialist voluntary organizations, he surfed its leftward eddies, never forming or leading a faction. He was handed a safe seat in the Illinois state senate, a nearly safe one in the U.S. Senate, and was surprised when Harry Reid informed him that influential Democrats wanted to run him for president. In short, Barack Obama himself is not that remarkable. He can give a rousing political speech, of course. Since he seems to have been reading from a teleprompter all his life, and since words certifiably his own are both few and opaque, it is most fruitful as well as relevant for us to focus on whom and what he has been following.

What accounts for his smooth, unlikely ascent? Both his advancement and his character seem most likely attributable to the network into which he was born, and out of which he never stepped for an instant. That network's privileges, wealth, and intellectual-social proclivities always depended to some extent on its connection with the U.S. government. Its intellectual and moral character has always been on the left side of American life and, in our time, combines upscale social norms with radical disdain for the rest of America. Barack Obama came of age through these. In sum, Barack Obama grew intertwined with the narrow, self-referential left side of the American Left. ... Their common problem, however, is that their agendas are antagonistic to people unlike themselves, and that they cannot keep from showing their contempt for the common folk in whose name they would ride to power. ... Obama is as close as one could imagine to a made-to-order front man for contemporary, upscale, *nouveau* socialism. A typical multiculturalist, Obama speaks no language other than a peculiar version of English. His native language, loves, and hates are common to some of the most leftist elements of the current American ruling class.[24]

Dick Morris has concerns that if President Obama is reelected to a second term, it will mean an increasing amount of soft despotism:

- Inflation will soar—not as a lamentable side effect of our government's policies, but because the government wants it and needs it. ... since that's the only way it can pay off its debt.
- The government will get the power to seize and reinvent any company it deems insolvent yet "too big to fail."
- Washington will set the standards that govern who gets lifesaving treatment or surgery ... and who is let to die. Government healthcare rationers will make the fateful decisions. They will balance cost against human life, ordering health providers to follow government protocols and prohibitions—even when it means an early death for tens of thousands of helpless elderly people.

- The top U.S. tax rate—combined with most states' rates—will reach more than half the income of the productive, entrepreneurial class—shriveling incentive and narcotizing ambition.[25]

> When Barack Obama arrived in Washington, our nation fell, unknowingly, into the grip of a committed socialist. ... Obama does not represent merely an alternative ideology or a different set of substantive priorities. He wants to change the basic philosophy and guiding principles of our nation—turning us into something we have never been, and that most of us don't want to become.... Obama's trans-formative presidency goes far deeper. ... He wants us to become dependent on government, to reduce our self-reliance, to curb our ambition, to narcotize ourselves with leisure, and to care more about the strangers we live among than the family for whom we are responsible. He is trying to seduce us with his offers of protection from cradle to grave. And, in return, he asks only that we sign over much of our freedom, our self-reliance, our ambition, and our initiative.[26]

Tyranny prevailed under some variation of the `"divine right of kings" for nearly 5,000 years. In addition, there was the reality that pure democracy can lead to majority `tyranny. After establishing a representative democracy, Tocqueville was among the first to utter warnings about the dangers of soft despotism. Now, the Democratic Party has the potential of `becoming the nucleus of a majority tyranny. Also, President Obama `has the potential to seduce America into a perpetual soft despotism.

In Part II, there will be an elaboration of how to resist and overcome these difficulties.

PART II:

REVERSING THE STATIST EROSION OF THE FEDERAL CONSTITUTION

In this Part II, the five chapters offer suggestions on how to deal with the problem of the progressive/statist erosion of the federal Constitution. First, everyone needs to know the enemy, to understand that this is political warfare, and that each side holds to fundamentally different expectations on the role of government. Both the Second and Tenth Amendments are necessary to preserve constitutional conservatism. Second, everyone must support efforts reform and reduce federal deficits, excessive government spending, and the national debt. Third, everyone must support reform of the federal tax code and have a higher percentage of Americans paying a share of the income tax. Fourth, everyone must support efforts to reclaim control over public education.

Finally, everyone needs to participate in the fight against an inevitable serfdom. At this time the Tea Party movement stands out as the best option to identify replacements for present members of the Cognoscenti. We today must be willing to pledge our life, fortune and sacred honor by electing to Congress representatives who will implement spending, taxation, and regulatory reforms that will correct the terrible erosion of our constitutional liberties.

5. BECOME A KNOWLEDGEABLE CITIZEN

Know the Enemy and Know Yourself

For those of us who are constitutional conservatives, the enemy is the Cognoscenti pursuing the progressive/statist agenda. This is a difference of kind, not a difference of degree. Repeat: it is a difference of *kind,* not of *degree.* It is not a matter of agreeing about the purpose or end of government, and then disagreeing about the means to achieve it. The disagreement is about the purpose. Either government exists to protect natural rights and remains limited or it exists to provide social justice, redistribute wealth, and become unlimited. There is no middle ground.

As explained by David Horowitz, the progressive/statists realize that they are engaged in political warfare. For the most part, constitutional conservatives are not engaged the same way. Sun Tzu wrote *The Art of War* in the sixth century BC. It has long been praised as the definitive work on military strategies. In it Sun Tzu observed winning a war required that one must first know the enemy. Constitutional conservatives must be keenly aware that the enemy are all those identified as the Cognoscenti who pursue the progressive/statist agenda.

In the 1930s Albert Jay Nock explained the difference between the State and government: "Nock argues that people can chose to interact in one of two ways, either by voluntary transactions or interactions, or by the use of force. He defines voluntary transactions as the 'economic means' of getting what we want and the use of force or theft as the 'political means.'

He defines the State (always in the upper-case) as the organization of the political means. Since the essence is force, fraud or violence, it is ever the enemy of humankind. Any strengthening of the State weakens society, the delicate interweaving of voluntary agreements that offers some hope for the development of civilization."[1]

From its beginnings, America did not have a formal aristocracy. Now we have a neo-aristocracy—the Cognoscenti—comprised of many elected politicians and government bureaucrats and constituting the ruling class. Of course not everyone elected to office or appointed to the bureaucracy is part of the Cognoscenti—just the ones who believe in progressivism with its underlying premise of statism. "America's government class has radically different interests from the rest of us—and it uses the power of government to further those interests. As J. P. Freire, writing for the *Washington Examiner*, put it, government today is 'not so much about haves and have nots. It's about haves and *have yours!*'"[2]

Consider what happened in Wisconsin in 2010, when the governor took steps to curtail the bargaining rights of public sector employees in order to get a handle on state expenditures:

> Unions, aided by their out-of-state comrades and President Obama's Organizing for America campaign group, are busing in thousands of supporters to storm the state capitol. The union supporters flood onto the Senate floor and throng the balcony. They chant, "This is what democracy looks like." Modern government serves itself; it has grown enormously, and its goal is to preserve and extend the powers and privileges of politicians, bureaucrats, and public-sector unions.[3]

Union members and the supposedly unorganized Occupy Wall Street movement used the tactics advocated by the radical Saul Alinsky in their demonstrations as explained by David Horowitz above. These demonstrations also cost money. Billionaire George Soros is a major contributor to statist causes. Readers can go online and research how his money has funded the Center for American Progress, Move On, the Democracy Alliance, the Open Society Institute, the Tides Foundation, and Media Matters. Soros reportedly has an agenda of one-world government and one currency that will solve world problems.

Many public servants declare war to "solve" every domestic crisis—much of which is caused by their "solutions" to earlier crises. Because many politicians are tempted to declare every problem a "war," this expanding government intervention in innumerable areas of our lives cannot stand up to careful examination. Here are three criticisms by syndicated columnists Rich Lowry, Victor David Hanson, and Thomas Sowell:

> The most striking fact about American politics is the disjunction between the opinions of ordinary Americans and the behavior of the political elites. Big government has become a cultural issue. All this has created the fear that something elemental was changing in the country—quickly, irrevocably, without notice. ... Obama is answering the call. Spending is sneaking up to European levels—an estimated 44 percent of GDP this year because politicians declare every problem a war—even before the baby boomers retire. He seeks to give us European-style health-care, energy and labor policies.[4]

> Americans still seethe about the Wall Street meltdown of 2008. But the "fat-cat bankers," in fact, were players in a far larger fraud made possible by liberal executives at Fannie Mae and Freddie Mac. Bill Clinton's appointees and insider friends like Franklin Raines, Jim Johnson, Jamie Gorelick, and Robert Rubin made millions while agencies and banks they oversaw lost billions. It was just disclosed that Rep. Barney Frank helped land a job at Fannie Mae for his the-live-in boyfriend Herb Moses—despite at the time sitting on a House oversight committee that monitored the federally regulated agency. Fannie Mae went belly

up. Moses made a lot of money. And Frank kept assuring the public in hearings that the nearly insolvent agency was in no financial danger. When news surfaced about Frank's conflict of interest, he scoffed, "There is no rule against it at all," and predicted the story would die. He was, right, it will. But substitute scary names like Dick Cheney or Halliburton and it would not have.[5]

When politicians think that they should be deciding how much money is enough for other people that is starting down a very slippery slope. Politicians with the power to determine each citizen's income are no longer public servants. They are public masters. ... But that is wholly different from having politicians make such decisions for other people. They drain away other people's money in order to hand out goodies that will help get themselves get reelected.[6]

Increase Knowledge of American Civics, History, Traditions

It's now our job to replenish the stocks of patriotism and belief in America; then we must pass them on to our children and to others who need guidance. To do this, it's necessary to read. We have to keep educating ourselves about the glory of America's history and about the facts of our freedom, prosperity, and moral leadership right now. Rather than go into detail here, I'll invite readers to examine the appendix for resources related to constitutional conservatism.

Keeping and Bearing Arms as a Barrier against Tyrannical Government

The Founding Fathers assumed a world where free men knew how to use firearms to provide for their families and to fight for them when necessary. One of the earliest exponents of the importance of keeping and bearing arms was Thomas Jefferson:

Jefferson said, "What country can preserve its liberties if its rulers are not warned from time to time that their people preserve the spirit of resistance? Let them take arms." The central component of the Second Amendment is to protect ourselves from the U.S. Congress, not street thugs.[7]

The Cognoscenti want to take away firearms in the name of public safety. They're shrill advocates of gun control. Now they want to control how much ammunition one may buy as well. The Second Amendment affirms this individual right, and this rests on an assumption of equivalence to police force weaponry. Weaponry of federal (and state and local) agencies now far exceeds that available to individuals; thus there is the danger of more tyranny. In Chicago there is an ongoing effort to control handguns: "Daley's not done on handguns…. The mayor is expected to demand registration of all handguns, mandatory training for gun owners and a limit of one handgun per person."[8]

In the recent *District of Columbia v. Heller* decision, the Supreme Court ruled 5-4 that the Second Amendment protects an individual's right to keep and bear arms. However it's troubling to read the arguments of the four who voted against this decision. They chose to focus on the "militia" purpose, and they completely ignored that the right to keep and bear arms was established in the English *Bill of Rights* (1689) and was part of the rights for which the Founding Fathers fought. Here is an excerpt from the minority opinion:

> In a dissenting opinion, joined by Justices David Souter, Ruth Bader Ginsburg, and Stephen Breyer, Justice John Paul Stevens said: "The Amendment's text does justify a different limitation: the 'right to keep and bear arms' protects only a right to possess and use firearms in connection with service in a state-organized militia. Had the Framers wished to expand the meaning of the phrase 'bear arms' to encompass civilian possession and use, they could have

done so by the addition of phrases such as 'for the defense of themselves.' "[9]

In my opinion, the Founders composed the amendment in a context of addressing the question of a standing army. They wanted each state to use its own militia. Unfortunately, modern day justices bring a worldview to their decision-making. They also bring great skill in the use of words and the use of research to back their arguments. Justice Stevens goes to great lengths to argue against a legal establishment enshrining the keeping and bearing arms for civilian in contrast to militia purposes. Unfortunately, he ignores the fundamental right that all of us are born with, namely, the right to life. That right means little, unless we simultaneously have the means to defend ourselves and protect the lives of our loved ones. This 5-4 decision underscores painfully just how perilously close we can come to losing our natural, God-given rights as long as justices can determine what the Constitution means.

Tenth Amendment Protection Against Tyrannical Federal government.

For thousands of years, people have tended to live with and work with people most like themselves, and this is explained by the rule of 150. Here are two observations about why people need the freedom to move from state to state rather than be confined within the limits of one, overall nation that administers all aspects of government:

> The favorite Democratic explanation is that the "red staters" are hicks who have been blinded by righteousness, and (middle-class Kansans) are so bamboozled by moral issues like abortion and school prayer that they vote for Republicans even though the GOP tax cutting is against their self-interest.[10]

Even today, if you separate people into different groups, they will quickly begin discriminating against others they deem unlike themselves. But middle-class Americans don't simply cast ballots for Republicans. They also vote with their feet, which is why blue states and old Democratic cities are losing population to red states and Republican exurbs. People are moving there precisely because of economic reasons—more jobs, affordable houses and the lower taxes offered by Republican politicians. Even today, as dozens of experiments have made clear, if you separate people into different groups—no matter how arbitrary the basis of the distinction—they will quickly begin discriminating against others they deem unlike themselves. People say they want to live in diverse integrated communities, but what they really want to do is live in homogenous ones, filled with people like themselves [the rule of 150]. Maybe the health of a society is measured by how freely people can move between institutions.[11]

From the beginning, each state retained responsibility for the health and safety of their citizens. In order to protect the state from invasion, it was necessary to have a militia, and that was composed of all able-bodied men being prepared to be part of the state militia. This requirement is now less necessary thanks to the modern paid National Guard. However, there is still the matter of whether the state or the Department of Defense commands the fundamental allegiance of the National Guard: "At the heart of the disagreement is who will command reserve troops when they go to a particular state to deal with a natural disaster."[12]

Another important reason for federalism is the absence of a national police force. From the beginning, the police power rested with the states that have locally elected sheriffs, district attorneys, and local police officers, and sheriff's deputies that all owe their primary allegiance to the municipality or the county and the state, not to the federal government. Again this is a stark contrast to most other major nations that have police power and court officers as a function of the national government. The *Posse Comitatus Act* (1878) prevents the federal government from turning the US military against its own citizens. The states act as a check on the potential tyranny of the federal government. "Be wary of using the military as police. The first concern was well-founded fears that the first attack would be on *Posse Comitatus*.... Every state's National Guard force is now equipped to cope with attacks using unconventional weapons."[13]

The main point of the Second Amendment is to remember that the natural right to life requires the means to preserve one's life, and the lives of loved ones, in the event of an attack by anyone with the possibility of losing one's life to the attacker. "We have been given the right to protect ourselves from danger, whether foreign or domestic. To give up that right is going against the well-reasoned intentions of our founding fathers. Another, even more important consideration is this: The founders expected citizens to be able to have guns as good as, or better than, the standard military operations of the time."[14] It is important to realize that in the aftermath of 9/11, many police and sheriff agencies now possess weapons equivalent to the military forces. This places them in a position of being able to "out-gun" the citizens they are appointed to protect.

In the coming year, it's important to remember that a president nominates members of the US Supreme Court who tend to share his worldview. If President Obama is reelected, he may have the opportunity to make two appointments to the highest court in the land. If they are similar to his appointment of justices Kagan and Sotomayor, then the progressives/statists will have a majority on the court, and this could have dire consequences for decades to come.

6. Reform government spending and reduce federal deficits

The Cognoscenti Spend to Redistribute Wealth

As America proceeds on the path to financial bankruptcy, neither political party has demonstrated serious concern about reducing annual spending; consequently, our national debt ceiling is constantly raised in order to borrow more money. At present the federal government borrows approximately $4 billion per day or approximately $1.3 trillion per year in order to meet spending commitments. Walter Williams and Robert Samuelson, two syndicated columnists, describe the broad implications of where this nation is heading:

> The rest of the federal government, including fighting two wars, homeland security, education, art, culture, you name it, veterans—the whole rest of the discretionary budget is being financed by China and other countries.[1]

> Spending is the crucial issue, because it determines taxes and deficits.... Until recently, the borrowings, though usually undesirable, were not alarming. But the recession and an aging population signify that we have crossed a threshold where actual and prospective borrowings are so huge that no one can foresee the consequences. ... Today's prospective colossal borrowings dwarf likely economic growth.[2]

Never before has our government borrowed this much money in peacetime. And now it's borrowing record amounts every year. The basic facts are these. The federal government is spending approximately $3.7 trillion and collecting revenues on the order of $2.3 trillion each year. In order to cover that deficit, the federal government is borrowing at the rate of $4 billion dollars a day, 365 days per year. Those loans require interest payments. At the present rate, interest payments on the debt will rise to the point of blocking out other much needed expenditures.

Entitlements Bankrupting the Nation

The United States is facing a severe demographics problem. There are not enough babies being born to enter the workforce to offset the increasing percentage of retired folks who are not only living longer but are expecting to have high-quality medical service at virtually no cost. To put the problem into perspective, here are excerpts from syndicated columnists Walter Williams, Morton Kondracke and Robert Samuelson:

> Today's federal budget is over $3 trillion dollars. I challenge anyone to find specific constitutional authority for at least $2 trillion of it. That includes Social Security, Medicare, farm and business handouts, education, prescription drugs and a host of other federal expenditures. Americans who have become accustomed to living at the expense of another American would not want Congress to obey the Constitution, especially if it left out their favorite handout.[3]

> Bush has already passed on to future generations the cost of his tax cuts—$5.7 trillion over 20 years.... His Social Security reforms would add $6 trillion over 20 years. The fact is that this generation's policy activists and political leaders have piled enormous burdens of debt on today's children and their children, and there's precious little sign that they plan to lighten it. The trustees of the Medicare system es-

timate that last year's prescription drug benefit plan alone will cost $8 trillion over the next 75 years. It was Bush's bill, backed by AARP as a "down payment" on an even richer benefit. Democrats opposed it as too small.[4]

To voters under age 35, you face a heavily mortgaged future. You'll pay the costs of Social Security and Medicare for aging baby boomers. The needed federal tax increase might total 50 percent over the next 25 years. Plus there's the expense of decaying infrastructure.... Pension and health costs for state and local workers have doubtlessly been underestimated. All this will squeeze other crucial government services: defense, police.[5]

Millions of Americans don't want their entitlement touched. Until recent years, Social Security recipients received more, often far more, than the value of the Social Security taxes they paid. Everyone who receives government largesse and special favors deems his needs as vital, deserving, proper and in the national interest. What's even worse for our nation is that voters ousting a politician who'd refuse to bring, say, aid to higher education back to his constituents is perfectly rational.... Once legalized theft begins, it pays for everyone to participate. Those who don't will be the losers. That's the nation's dilemma. The most important job for people who want to spare our nation from economic collapse is to convince our fellow Americans to respect the limits of our Constitution.[6]

The Cognoscenti Avoid Dealing with the Deficit and Debt

At present, the federal debt is $16 trillion and is expected to grow by a trillion or more each year for the next decade. Syndicated columnist David

Brooks points to the intellectual deficit of the American Cognoscenti as he reviews what has happened to similar governmental programs in Europe:

> Events in Western Europe are discrediting large swaths of American liberalism [progressive/statist agenda]. Europe has enacted generous welfare measures, ample labor protections, highly progressive tax rates, single-payer health care systems, zoning restrictions to limit big retailers and cradle-to-grave middle-class subsidies supporting everything from child care to pension security. Far from thriving, continental Europe has endured a lost decade of relative decline.... Unemployment has been stuck between 8 and 11 percent since 1991 and growth has reached 3 percent only once in those 14 years. ...The core fact is that the European model is foundering under the fact that billions of people [in other parts of the world] are willing to work harder than the Europeans are. ... Over the last few decades, American liberals [progressive/statists] have lauded the German model or the Swedish model or the European model. ... These models encourage people to cling fiercely to entitlements their nation cannot afford. ... They breed a reactionary fear of the future that lashes out ferociously at anybody who proposes fundamental reform or at any group, like immigrants, that alters the fabric of life. This is the chief problem with the welfare state that it breeds a stultifying fear of dynamic flexibility, a greater concern for guarding what exists than for creating what doesn't.[7]

Currently at least two proposals are available for fundamental reform: the National Commission on Fiscal Responsibility and Reform and the Debt Reduction Task Force of the Bipartisan Policy Center. Currently, both proposals languish on the sidelines.

Ever since the conclusion of World War II, both major political parties have avoided the necessity of raising taxes by borrowing money. What that has done over the seven decades is to have a persistent devaluation of the dollar and an increasing level of inflation. The reality of inflation is such that the burden falls mainly on those with the least ability to pay—those on fixed incomes and the truly impoverished.

> As Henry Hazlitt points out, it is foolish to think that government can create "wealth" by borrowing money and "investing" it into the economy, since the debt will eventually have to be repaid. Printing additional money creates inflation, which harms businesses and individuals, depreciating the value of their savings, and creating an uncertain economic environment.... Subsidies must be paid for, and government can only raise money through taxation.[8]

Both major parties vote consistently to increase the debt limit. Originally the intent was to borrow money and increase the debt only in the case of a national emergency, then pay it back from future tax revenues. Instead the idea of emergency has been transformed into some sort of status quo. This means ever more borrowing and increasing erosion of the value of the dollar. Both political parties are guilty of increasing the debt limit and this must stop unless it is a matter of national emergency. More than anything else, curtailing the erosion in the value of the dollar and America's perceived number-one status in the financial world should be a primary goal.

Eight Recommendations to Regain Control of Government

Ian Murray, mentioned in chapter 3, provides eight suggestions for action that would enable constitutional conservatives to reclaim control of the federal government:

1. Shrink the federal government. Eliminate four departments: Commerce, Education, Energy, and Labor.

There needs to be an immediate and radical reduction in the size of government and its functions. Whole departments need to be swept away [starting with] the Department of Commerce, which is where Big Government started. ... Also on the chopping block should be the Departments of Energy, Labor and Education.... Meanwhile, the Department of Education could better be titled the Department of Misallocating Education Dollars, as its real function appears to be that of a vacuum that sucks up taxpayer dollars to distribute to fellow education bureaucrats around the country—who then put their own interests ahead of our children's interests.[9]

2. Reform federal pay and conditions.

We need to overhaul how federal workers are paid: automatic pay raises need to go, as do seniority-based pay scales, and the virtual immunity of federal workers from being fired. We need to get back to the idea of "public service" where government workers—on the public payroll—don't make more than taxpayers in comparable jobs. Unaffordable government pension schemes should be passed out and replaced by a 403(b) plan—the non-profit version of the 401(k).[10]

3. End labor union privileges.

It is frankly ridiculous that people can be forced to pay dues to a union of which they aren't members, but from Wisconsin teachers to public employees across the country, this is often the case. The first thing to do is to remove public sector union collective bargaining privileges. ... But in the event that Congress is too cowardly to act ... state and local governments should take the lead in revoking collective bargaining agreements. This will be met with ferocious opposition, as happened in Wisconsin, but it is a necessary step in reforming public sector pay and benefit arrangements. ... Congress should repeal actions by the National Labor Relations Board (NLRB) that make it easier for unions to organize without the approval of a majority of the workers.[11]

4. Tackle entitlement spending (Social Security, Medicare, and Medicaid).

A tiny number of Americans pay for the well being of nearly a majority. While half of the population may pay something in taxes, only the top 10%—people earning more than $113,000—pay a substantive amount. These few citizens pay 70% of all the income taxes collected. Benefits funded this way are unsustainable. According to a recent study published in the *Wall Street Journal*, the average couple that retires at age 66 on Social Security and Medicare will receive $1 million in benefits. On average, they and their employers paid $500,000 into the system. The federal government is taking an excessive amount of money from its few high earners—a wealthy minority —and redistributing it inefficiently to pay for services the country can't realistically afford. ... America's entitlement programs (most notably Social Security, Medicare, and Medicaid) are the product of a very different America, where it was assumed that the elderly were at particular risk of falling into poverty. Seniors today are among the wealthiest people in America; and though entitlements once given are hard to take away, the simple fact is that elderly Americans have no need for universal entitlements. Moreover, our government can't afford it. Life expectancy has increased sharply, meaning that more seniors acclaiming more benefits for longer than the system can possibly sustain.[12]

5. Make contracts public and abolish grants.

The Office of Personnel Management should be required to find out how many people government contractors employ on a government contract; and the Office for Management and Budget should have the power to revoke contracts that are poor value for the money; this would expose the "shadow government" of government contactors to light. Research grants should be abolished because they reward ideas for research rather than the results of research, and are easily abused for patronage.... Science will be less skewed by political considerations and much more dedicated to finding scientific solutions to public problems.[13]

6. Privatize appropriate government functions.

Many state and local public sector services might be better handled by the private or voluntary sector. Many local fire departments, for instance, are already run by private companies. Prisons, too, are often run on a private basis and have generally improved conditions for prisoners. Private schools have a long history of outperforming public schools—often at a far lower cost.… Neighborhood associations have been privatizing what had been the provinces of municipal government, de facto creating their own zoning laws and taking over services like snow removal, garbage collection, and so on, an providing such amenities as community swimming pools, golf courses, and landscaping. There are two obstacles to overcome: one, the threat of "double taxation" from local government and neighborhood association fees, and, two, the lack of simple arrangements for such associations to form where local government is entrenched.[14]

7. Re-charter executive agencies.

There are some agencies that are mightier than the government departments, such as the Environmental Protection Agency and the Food and Drug Administration. These should be reined in by reducing their regulatory powers and by new congressional charters strictly enumerating what they can do—and the level of service to be provided to the taxpayer. Enforcement should be left to district attorneys, courts, and due process. No agency should ever treat an American citizen as a potential criminal rather than as a customer worthy of respect. The bureaucracy works best that is entitled to do the least.[15]

8. Enact regulatory reform.

Congress needs to reassert control over the bureaucratic regulators. [Congress needs to pass a law that] would require a congressional go-ahead for any major regulation that would impose significant costs on the economy. … Other measures (suggested by Wayne Crews and Ryan Young) include: Appoint an annual bipartisan commission to comb through the books and suggest rules that deserve repeal. Require all new regulations to have built-in five-year sunset provisions. Propose that for every new rule that hits the books, an old one must be repealed. Finally, in no cases should agencies be allowed to be both judge and jury when it comes to any of their powers. We have seen how the EPA is tasked both to compile the science on global warming and then to assess whether the results are accurate and whether they demand action.... The bureaucrats don't merit this power; the people's representatives, Congress, should decide.[16]

Since 1995 the federal government has issued more than 60,000 regulations, all with the force of law. The Federal Register runs to some 60,000-70,000 pages each year.[17]

In 2005, the Small Business Administration (estimated) that complying with regulation cost the economy $1.1 trillion in 2004, when our GDP was $11 trillion.[18]

This concludes the suggestions on how to deal with the problems of excessive government spending and the continual increase of the national debt. In the next chapter, the companion topic of taxation will be examined.

7. REFORM THE FEDERAL TAX CODE AND INCREASE REVENUES

Those holding to the progressive/statist agenda realized perhaps their greatest triumph when they used populist arguments against the super-rich (the "robber barons") of the early twentieth century, and they gained enough support to pass the Sixteenth Amendment, which installed a national income tax. By 1913, enough states had ratified the amendment that it became effective during Woodrow Wilson's first year in office. Since then, larger and larger amounts of money have flowed to Washington, and the politicians and bureaucrats cannot seem to exhaust the different ways that they want to spend it.

From 1913 to 2005, the income tax has enabled, entitled, empowered, and engorged the federal government, and states, and local governments. Spending has grown by more than 13,592 percent. The income tax gives the federal government a blank check to spend money, even money it does not yet have. The federal government lays a claim on all future economic activity of its citizens; its massive debts are a lien on the earnings of people who have not yet even drawn their first breaths.

> In 2010, by using its police power to tax, the government controlled over 40 percent of our country's financial resources (i.e. spending by federal, state and local government as a percent of annual gross domestic product).... With almost 50 percent of all U.S. households excused from paying federal income taxes, and a large proportion of the rest content with the statist philosophy that is pervasive

among our government leaders, personal sacrifice for the cause seems almost an act of martyrdom.[1]

Along the way, the federal tax code has become a monstrosity littered with exceptions and loopholes that are intended to benefit special interests. Here are three perspectives by syndicated columnists Walter Williams, Thomas Sowell, and George F. Will:

> The tax code has grown to gargantuan proportions, as individuals and special interest groups have employed highly skilled attorneys and accountants to manipulate the code to their optimum advantage. It's not just rich people who try to avoid taxes, but all of us—liberals, conservatives and libertarians. What is the evidence? Federal tax collections have been between 15 and 20 percent of the nation's GDP every year since 1960. However, between 1960 and today, the top marginal tax rate has varied between 19 and 35 percent. That means whether taxes are high or low, people make adjustment in their economic behavior so as to keep the government tax take between 15 and 20 percent of the GDP.... So far as Congress' ability to prey on the rich, we must keep in mind that rich people didn't become rich by being stupid.[2]

> What are called "tax cuts for the rich" have been reductions in high tax rates under four different administrations. ... The rich have ended up paying both a higher total amount of taxes and a larger share of all taxes than they did before what were called "tax cuts for the rich." The reason is very straightforward: high tax rates that people don't actually pay do not bring the government as much revenue as lower tax rates that they do pay. High tax rates drive investors into tax shelters or drive their investments out of the country altogether, costing Americans jobs.[3]

Because taxophobia is the strongest political passion today, some liberals believe the flow of Social Security tax dollars is necessary for domestic spending programs. But liberals cannot remain liberals and remain collaborators in the current process whereby Social Security revenues are used for the slow, surreptitious semirepeal of a great liberal achievement: the 16th Amendment, and the heavy reliance on the income tax. That has been happening, with the connivance of a Democratic-controlled Congress. … What the "Reagan revolution" changed radically is the incidence of taxation. Income taxes were cut and made less progressive. The regressive Social Security tax rate (the same rate for all payers; and income above $51,300 is exempt) increased 2 percent in the 1980s. Now the burden of the Social Security tax (including the employer's share) is larger than the income-tax burden for 74 percent of all taxpayers.[4]

Milton Friedman argued the case for having a flat tax:

In our book *Capitalism and Freedom* (1962), we recommended as a substitute for the existing personal income tax "a flat-rate tax on income above an exemption, with income defined very broadly ad deductions allowed only for strictly defined expenses of earning income." In 1962, this suggestion was dismissed as radical, impractical, and visionary. But circumstances alter cases. … Simultaneously, the public became more cynical about the income tax. "Soak the rich" has retained its demagogic appeal, but the conviction that the existing highly graduated income tax does in fact "sock the rich" has eroded sharply. … In a true flat-rate tax, a rate of not more than 15 or 16 percent would yield the same revenue as the present system with its rates of 12 to 50 percent, assuming present personal exemptions were retained. If allowing for the affect of inflation on exemptions a somewhat higher rate, perhaps 17 percent, would be required to raise the same revenue.[5]

Author Ian Murray also recommends introducing a single fair tax.

> The first step to tax reform is recognizing that income should be taxed only once. At present we are taxed on our money when we earn it, when we try to save or invest it, when we purchase something and when we try to leave it to our heirs on our death. ... Death taxes, capital gains taxes, and other additional taxes on our earnings should be abolished. What should take their place is a single, flat income tax where all income is taxed once, with everyone paying the same rate, with the revenues then being split between federal, state, and local government. Seven states ... and many Eastern European countries already operate under a flat tax; so we know it can work. A flat-tax could even serve as a social welfare program that avoids the problem of means testing (where people can be discouraged from earning more income because it will cost them benefits).[6]

Although it would be preferable to repeal the Sixteenth Amendment, it is unlikely that could happen today. There are too many vested interests that now support the idea of a national income tax. Yet, if one thinks about it, it is a clear violation of our natural right to the pursuit of happiness. The income tax allows the government to take your property, money, and then turn it around and give it to others either in the form of direct payments or indirectly in expenditures that may or may not be of benefit to you. Therefore, in order to reverse the path toward financial ruin that has been paved by the progressive/statist agenda, it is imperative to elect politicians who will commit to implementing the reforms discussed above.

All the while making efforts to control excessive spending, increasing debt, and a taxation system badly in need of reform, the other side - the Cognoscenti – continues to recruit new members from among graduates that have been indoctrinated in American colleges, universities and public high schools. Thus, Chapter 8 describes a companion effort to simultaneously strive to reclaim control over American public education.

8. Reclaim control over public education

Federal control of public education preempts local and state governments.

As described in chapter 3, the agenda of the Cognoscenti is aided and abetted within academia, and indoctrination takes place in classrooms that yield more recruits to swell the ranks of the Cognoscenti. This is largely a consequence of two events. First the federal income tax funnels a stream of money to the federal government, which puts the states in the position of supplicants to obtain their "fair share" for ongoing budget needs. Second conflict with the USSR during the Cold War years stimulated the idea that the federal government had to fund education programs, particularly in the sciences and engineering, in the name of national security. That reason no longer exists. With the federal money available and flowing into the colleges and universities, all other fields of study have piggy-backed onto the mathematics, technology, engineering and science departments so they too can receive research funding, grants-in-aid for faculty members, and financial loan programs for students.

The result is a situation in which the federal government through the Department of Education has created a monstrous bureaucracy that seeks any means possible to sustain itself. Ian Murray, who was educated in Great Britain, provides a scathing view of the American education establishment:

The idea that government had to be involved in scientific research started with Vannevar Bush (the top scientific advisor
to FDR) and gained credence because of the need for mil-
itary-driven research in World War II and, later, the Cold
War. Adam Smith had long before demonstrated, most
technological advances actually arise within industry. ...
Smith rejected the idea that applied sciences should be supported by the state, because market forces did a much more
efficient job. Smith's faith in the market, rather than government, as the driver of most technological advances has been
vindicated by empirical studies covering the 1960s, 1970s,
and the mid-1980s, which showed that only about 10 percent of industrial advances required academic research. ...
Government is singularly ill-suited for promoting scientific
research, because it is driven by political rather than practical considerations—and politicians, as a rule, are both bad
judges of commercial opportunity and ignorant of science.
What really drives political decisions are special interest
groups and electoral constituencies. The goal in politics
is to get reelected, and large projects are almost inevitably
awarded as pork barrel grants (regardless of actual need)....
Bureaucrats who take unpopular stands may later find it difficult to secure lucrative positions in the private sector.[1]

Many faculty are inclined to share the worldview of the progressive/
statist agenda, and that contributes to the inertia of trying to roll back the
presently distorted public education system. Larry Schweikart and Michael
Allen express their view of the academic landscape as they see it today:

Where will the competition come from in the university system? The universities are essentially isolated
and immunized from competition.... There are a lot of
new Internet universities out there. ... Do I see a lot
of conservative Hillsdale College, Grove City Colleges,

or Claremont colleges out there? Not really. ... There are conservative professors, but they're in the business schools, the engineering schools, and in the sciences. All the ultra liberals are in the arts, humanities, history, political science, sociology, ethnic studies and so on.[2]

Two of the major changes in the American economy are the upward trend in the number of individuals with college degrees and the declining trend of jobs that require only a high school diploma or less. Consequently, the number of jobs available that truly require a college degree is shrinking. This brings into question the cost-benefit ratio of spending a great deal of time and money to acquire a degree when it's becoming less relevant to obtain a well-paying, meaningful career. In an op ed piece, Gary Jason makes clear that the costs of a college degree in the form of loans may be a poor investment for many Americans:

> The percentage of American adults (ages 25-34) with college degrees is now 40.4 percent. From 1993-2007 enrollment at the top 198 public and private universities went up by 14.5 percent and the tuition those students paid increased by 66.7 percent. These top universities have more full-time employees devoted to administration than those employed to carry out the core function of teaching.[3]

Take steps to curtail federal responsibility for education.

Murray makes the case that it's past time to reengineer education. As for higher education, the financial aid system needs to be radically overhauled, and funding of public universities needs to be revised to reflect performance.... At both university and secondary levels, it is necessary to restore both the textbooks and teaching of American traditions.

For those institutions and faculty that accept public tax money, create appropriate outside influence on the selection, promotion and recognition of professors to amend the present system where faculty only determines who is hired, promoted, receives tenure, and gets published.

Work to find ways to modify curriculum (humanities, social sciences) with crack pot ideas that serve to indoctrinate the students.

Work to amend the balance of faculty with differing worldviews, particularly in the humanities and social sciences.

> That means, if universities receive public funds they need to be responsible to the taxpayer, college should not be a four-, five-, six- or seven-year party leaving students with a mountain of debt at the end. ... State governments might also want to consider shifting their resources away from universities to vocational schools where the cost-benefit ratio might be more direct. Finally, ending union collective bargaining agreements and replacing tenure with long-term contracts, as happened in the UK, should help rebalance lecturers' compensation arrangements and still secure academic freedom.[4]

The Department of Education has been a matter of questionable necessity for decades. However, like other bureaucratic institutions, the Cognoscenti have defended their turf against all attempts to reduce or abolish the mission of the department. Because the money flows to Washington, it provides the bureaucrats with the opportunity to give positive incentives in the forms of grants-in-aid, and it has taken on the role of policing local education by the implementation of standardized testing. Dan Walters, George Will, Evers and Wurnan, and Thomas Sowell take on the topics of spending on education and the results of standardized testing:

> The graduation rate for American high schools in 2003 was 70 percent, ranging from 88 percent in New Jersey to 54 percent in South Carolina. African Americans—55%, Latino—53%. Girls of all races did significantly better than boys.[5]

> The federal and state governments continue to scam the public into believing student performance in the nation's

public schools is improving. "There is very little correlation between the amount of money a state spends on public education and how its students fare in academic tests, dropout rates and other measures of educational performance. … There is very little correlation between the amount of money a state spends on public education and how its students fare in academic tests, dropout rates and other measures of educational performance.[6]

The law should have set uniform standards and measures for the nation, then freed states, districts and schools to produce those results as they think best. Instead, it left standards up to the states, which have an incentive to dumb them down to make compliance easier.[7]

During summer 2010, the California Academic Standards Commission (where we were members who voted in opposition) recommended the adoption of the federally promoted national standards. … (California) tried to grasp both horns of the dilemma, leaving us with a plan that could work only on paper. … The newly adopted plan expects teachers to teach and eighth graders to learn in one year both pre-algebra and Algebra I. The emptiness of this double-whammy option will hamper the future success of California students—disadvantaged students in particular. The rule-making, rule-enforcement, standards-writing, and standards adoption constraints of the federal government sabotaged the steady progress in math achievement of California students.[8]

If the students don't reach the standards, bring the standards down to them. Meanwhile, the education establishment has developed a whole inventory of tactics for responding to critics with excuses, evasions and verbal counterattacks.[9]

Reassert Citizen Control of School Boards

When America was founded, schooling was a local responsibility. Parents would get together and hire a schoolmaster to teach their children the three Rs. To this day members of the Amish church have schooling through the eighth grade and maintain that's all that's necessary for folks who are primarily farmers. Unfortunately farming and manufacturing have receded; they're no longer primary occupations. Instead, we have white-collar jobs and both parents typically work them. This means that parental control and participation in local school boards have declined markedly. In recent years, Congress has passed laws that have set national standards for educational outcomes. This has produced mixed results:

> [Education Secretary Arne Duncan] insists that it is irrational to have 50 goal posts. Allowing states to define academic proficiencies, while federal policy gives financial rewards for achieving those proficiencies, produces perverse incentives. If there must be federal education policy, then encourage 50 laboratories of educational experimentation. Federal policy should be confined to providing financial rewards contingent on improvements confirmed by national metrics.[10]

Local school boards are increasingly made up of teachers or persons employed by the education system. This tends to skew outcomes not only for pay and benefits but also for the curriculum. Unless and until more parents are willing to take time to serve on local school boards, it will be very difficult to overcome the inertia of the present status quo dominated by the Cognoscenti.

Competition Provides Parents More Choices

Third, competition among local schools for students would provide parents more choices, such as charter schools, voucher programs, and so forth. We need to establish curriculum review boards with more parental input. Here are excerpts from Walter Williams and Ben Stein:

> The solution to America's education problems … is the introduction of competition that could be achieved through school choice. Most people agree there should be public financing of education, but there is absolutely no case to be made for public production of education.[11]

> Nothing will do more to end our current paralysis than changing what our children are being taught. If I had to choose between winning control of the US Senate, and winning control of our country's local school boards—I'd choose the school boards. … All of the above applies to the college level as well. There's no reason not to write to your children's instructors and ask them to consider using some of the books you've read that will instill pride in our nation. If the professor mocks and then ignores you—a real possibility in today's universities—then offer the books to your child/student yourself with a request that he or she read them. Not all children belittle all that's suggested to them by their parents. Take a chance.[12]

John Stossel has made a career out of examining waste and fraud within all aspects of government. He is concerned about what is occurring in American education, and he makes these suggestions:

> Also, take a hand in your children's education. Ask to see the list of books that will be studied in their history, world civilization, civics, and English classes. If they're all anti-American and anti-freedom books that mock and belittle our country, suggest some alternatives. If you feel that you've read or experienced enough to be able to talk to the

students at your nearby school, volunteer to be a speaker about some aspect of the United States experience that you know well. This is a particularly apt suggestion for current and former military men and women. ... You know about your interests better than the education bureaucrats.[13]

To conclude this section, Vicki Murray, John Stossel, Star Parker and Alan Bonsteel make recommendations for reclaiming control over American public education:

By a margin of almost 9 to 1, Californians say that more money alone is not the answer to school improvement. ... If they truly seek to restore excellence in California education, the governor, his committee and legislators mustn't confuse more resources alone with reform. A good start would be replacing the state's ossified regulatory bureaucracy with research-based, student-centered reforms that let parents choose their children's schools.[14]

There are two means of improving public education by providing alternatives. One, give parents vouchers to use at any school, private or public. Second, allow parents more choices of charter schools. The unions representing teachers, administrators, and other employees in the public education system have resisted both of these options. That yet another court rejected the favorite legal claims of school choice opponents should give heart to proponents of equal educational opportunity nationwide.[15]

In other words, voucher money is a foot in the door for the "educrats." [Stossel could have used *Cognoscenti*.] If vouchers contain this potential danger, what can be done to help get kids out of dismal government schools? A better alternative is a tax credit for any parent who pays for private schooling or anyone else who helps put children through nongovernmental schools.[16]

Public school proposed reforms are rejected by the unions. Problems today in the inner cities are complex. Many poor families are broken, single-parent homes…. Kids from these homes get sent to public schools where prohibitions on providing any framework for values make it impossible to help them find meaning amidst the chaos in which they live. It doesn't take much imagination to predict where this leads. We can educate these kids. But we need to open the education market place, take it out of the hands of the unions and monopolists.[17]

However, "fully funding" our public schools has never meant fair funding for our public charter schools, which outperform traditional public schools with only about three-quarters of the per-student funding.[18]

Opposition from Teachers' Unions and other Labor Organizations

Once this effort to reclaim control over public education commences, prepare for active, intense opposition from teachers' unions and other labor and community organizations Murray observes the positive consequences of ending collective bargaining agreements and replacing tenure with long-term contracts as happened in the UK. In his opinion, this helped rebalance teachers' compensation arrangements and still secured for them academic freedom. He makes a similar observation concerning America:

Ending collective bargaining arrangements and abolishing federal education programs will go a long way to reforming education. Equally fundamental is giving parents more choices on where they send their children to school. The local state school should not hold monopoly power over parents; state schools should have to compete for students. Wherever "school choice" has been tried—most notably in Sweden—it has been a significant success, reducing costs and bureaucracy while providing better quality education.[19]

In many larger school districts, such as in the City of Los Angeles, educational unions exert an enormous influence over school board members. In the Los Angeles school district, traditional educational policy is not effective and almost half the students drop out. "And the unions still fabricate the issues to destroy these progressive plans of needed change, as clearly seen in 2005 in California with Gov. Schwarzenegger's failed slate of referenda."[20]

On the federal level, the National Education Association (NEA) is a stout defender of the status quo. "The NEA, the giant dinosaur of educational policy, is the largest single reason why the public-school system seems almost impervious to real reform. Its clear goal is power over a monopolistic system, and it will do whatever it must to retain that power."[21]

> Education is too important to be left to the union-government monopoly.
>
> School spending in America (adjusted for inflation) has more than tripled over the past 30 years, but national test scores are flat. The average per-pupil cost today is an astonishing $10,000 per student—$200,000 per classroom! Think how many teachers you could hire, and how much better you could do with that much money.[22]

Many Americans are coming to realize that unions and collective bargaining rights for public-sector employees have very undesirable consequences. They ignore several realities. In the private sector, if an employee cannot reach an agreement with his or her employer on compensation and benefits, the employee can refuse to work—he or she can go on strike. The employer, in turn, can lock his or her doors and shut out the employee. In the public sector, those tactics make no sense. Further we must remember that most public-sector workers have had some form of civil service protection going all the way back to the Pendleton Act of 1883. These protections are still in place; collective bargaining rights are layered on top of them.

Finally there's the matter of who is the employer and by what method are they chosen. In the private sector, the board of directors is the employer. Employees have absolutely no say as to how they are selected. The board is responsible to the stockholders and other investors. In the public sector, the city council or the local school board is the employer. They are selected by voting citizens. They are responsible to the citizens for providing certain goods and services. Employees, as citizens, can vote for candidates running for council member or school board member. Through employee unions, support for particular candidates can have strong influence on the outcome of an election. So, unlike the private sector, public employees can campaign for and help elect the equivalent of a board of directors, that is, a city council or a school board. Employees in the public sector, by electing favored candidates, can influence employer decisions regarding pay, benefits and working conditions. Generally, the American public tends to overlook the significance of this, particularly when public employees demonstrate and say all they want are the same rights as exist for private sector union members. This, of course, is a vast charade.

The predictable organized resistance by labor organizations to these suggestions will only be a subset of the predictable outcry and demonstrations to changing the status quo on government spending and taxation policies. In recent years, such attempts at government austerity within the European Union (Greece, Spain, France, Italy and Portugal) spawned massive protests. Television coverage displayed fighting with police, burning of automobiles, smashing of store windows, and other displays of barbaric behavior. No one can expect anything less to happen here in America, unless and until it is made clear that we are all in the same boat, and we are all heading for a perilous waterfall. Chapter 9 makes clear that it is a matter of how willing we are to pull together to avoid this calamity.

9. Fight to avoid an inevitable serfdom

On the Road to Serfdom

Within the last seven or eight decades there has been a slow, hardly noticed psychological change in the electorate. Americans are becoming too used to the welfare state and are out of practice in protesting the loss of their liberties. Recognizing this same tendency many decades ago, Friedrich von Hayek wrote *The Road to Serfdom* (1944) and raised concerns about the psychological change brought about by extensive government control that impacts political ideals and political institutions. After its publication, he said people missed the main point of his book, which was:

> that the most important change that extensive government control produces is a psychological change, an alteration in the character of the people. This is necessarily a slow affair, a process that extends not over a few years but perhaps over one or two generations. The important point is that the political ideals of a people and its attitude toward authority are as much the effect as the cause of the political institutions under which it lives. This means, among other things, that even a strong tradition of political liberty is no safeguard if the danger is precisely that new institutions and policies will gradually undermine and destroy that spirit. The consequences can of course be averted if that spirit

reasserts itself in time and the people not only throw out the party that has been leading them further and further in the dangerous direction but also recognize the nature of the danger and resolutely change their course.[1]

Back in chapter 3, Dick Morris reminded us about "plantation masters."

Our modern plantation owners—people with unimaginable wealth—have no qualms in using the money of the middle class to buy the votes of the poor and do not worry about how these very taxes will block the middle classes' upward mobility. The rich men and women who have now become our senators, congressmen, governors, cabinet officers, and presidents use the power their money has bought them to buy off the masses with programs, and to enfeeble the upper middle class with taxes.[2]

The observations of Hayek and Morris prompted thoughts about how serfdom compares to slavery. Generally serfs were tied to the land and could not be bought, sold, or traded as individuals. They voluntarily agreed to work their land and the land of the lord of the manor in exchange for protection against robbers and other invaders. By comparison, slaves were part of a system called chattel slavery. They were there involuntarily and were forced to do any work ordered by the plantation owner. Since they could be bought or sold, they had the same status as a horse, plow, or other piece of personal property.

In making a comparison between the practice of slavery of yesteryear and the voluntary serfdom that is present today, let us consider five elements of comparison: the slaves, the rulers, the plantations, the community, and the opponents.

The slaves. Slaves were brought to America in involuntary bondage. They only could have what the owners allowed. Today, we have serfs who are in voluntary bondage. In place of plantation owners, the Cognoscenti now provide social safety nets and other forms of government assistance.

Modern day serfs are people being seduced into voluntary bondage by receiving government checks (social security, Medicare, welfare, veterans' benefits, disability benefits, educational grants-in-aid, and research money, etc.); receiving some form of monetary benefit (mortgage loan deductions, business expense write offs, tax credits, etc.) or benefiting from a law or regulation put in place for a special interest group (affirmative action, union membership protections, tariffs, anti-competition protections, etc.).

The rulers. The plantation owners were the economic ruling class. Overseers who used whips and dogs to keep the slaves in line assisted them. Today, the Cognoscenti are the political ruling class. In place of overseers, these politicians and bureaucrats have enforcement officials who use regulations, fines, threats of tax audits, confiscating rosewood from a guitar manufacturer; or an NLRB ruling to prevent Boeing from relocating a plant to South Carolina. All these actions are intended to keep modern day serfs in line.

The plantations. Previously, plantations were tangible pieces of property with buildings and other structures. They were readily recognizable. Today, in place of recognizable plantations, there are no tangible visible structures that bring to consciousness the condition of the modern equivalency of serfdom present throughout American society.

The community. Previously, the community upheld the system of slavery, because of the benefits received from money spent by the owners after the crop was sold. They were unconcerned with the slaves, who were viewed a sub-human. Today, we have a community made up of judges, lobbyists, consultants, public sector union leaders, journalists, entertainers in New York and Hollywood, academics and businessmen who benefit from participation in the progressive/statist status quo. They are unconcerned with modern day serfs, those who are in bondage to the notion of redistributed wealth and equality of outcomes. They are losing their freedom bit by bit, and they become casualties of this subtle warfare to take from those who earn and redistribute wealth, in the name of social justice, in order to achieve a utopia here on earth.

The opponents. Abolitionists who viewed slave holding as morally reprehensible and others who were indifferent to the idea of slavery lived outside the slave-holding region. At that time, their efforts met such resistance that only a civil war could resolve the conflict. Today, Lincoln's idea of an "apple of gold" should prompt constitutional conservatives to fight against the conditions of modern serfdom. It will not be easy, for once individuals are accustomed to the benefits distributed by the Cognoscenti, it becomes like an addiction that is difficult to eradicate. However, all of these programs and benefits were voted into existence at one time. Now, it will take courageous representatives to either vote to reduce their impact or to eliminate them entirely.

The Tea Party Movement Can Unseat the Cognoscenti

The Tea Party movement emerged in 2009 as a response to the federal government's 2008 bailouts and passage of the 2009 stimulus package. A series of protests were organized around the theme of TEA (standing for *taxed enough already*). It wasn't long before this protest against too much government spending was linked back to the historic events that resulted in the Boston Tea Party of 1773, the prelude to the American War of Independence. William Voegeli provides this insight into the origins of the Tea Party movement:

> One point about the tea party movement is not in dispute: it was triggered on the morning of February 19, 2009, by Rick Santelli on CNBC. "How many of you people want to pay for your neighbor's mortgage who has an extra bathroom and can't pay their bills?" Getting more worked up, Santelli said, "We're thinking about having a Chicago tea party in July. All of you capitalists that want to show up to Lake Michigan, I'm going to start organizing it." Santelli, it turned out, didn't need to do any organizing, or to wait five months for people to take action. The Tea Party movement was born. CNBC and YouTube viewers launched websites and Facebook pages within hours of the rant heard 'round the world.[3]

Other claims to being the first to emerge include activist Mary Rakovich, who organized a February 10, 2009, protest in Fort Myers, Florida, calling it the "first protest of President Obama's administration that we know of." Seattle blogger and conservative activist Keli Carender is credited also as organizing Tea Party style protests in February of 2009. "Instead of New Deal-style acclamation, Obama's orgy of state-building has been greeted by an entirely new grassroots conservative movement, the Tea Party, as well as a firming and inspiriting of right-wing public opinion across the board."[4]

The Tea Party movement could also be described as the "Leave us Alone Coalition" mentioned above in chapter 2. Collectively, they believe in the same principles that motivated the Founding Fathers. They don't want other people's money; they don't want other people taking their money. They want to start businesses without being overtaxed and over-regulated. They want to educate their children where and how they see fit. Opinion writer Martin Wishek spells out an imperative:

> We must vote out of office those politicians who espouse the liberal [progressive/statist] views that have gotten us into our current sorry state of affairs. We must elect those who want to cut back the size of government, reduce and reform unsustainable entitlements, eliminate inefficient programs, and remove unnecessary rules and regulations that strangle business. If we don't we are destined for a dismal future. The liberals' [Progressives] dream will become America's nightmare.[5]

The Tea Party movement reasserts the same spirit that motivated the American colonists in 1774 when they organized committees of correspondence. The purpose was to share information among the thirteen colonies and to coordinate action in response to the increasingly tyrannical behavior of the British government. In like manner, there are now Tea Party chapters in all fifty American states. It is vitally important that this movement not become seduced into the trap of creating a national organization and employing full-time staff to run the organization. One of the bedrock necessities to protect our rights is to preserve federalism, that is, the separate and distinct responsibilities of the fifty sovereign states. In that manner, it will always be a barrier to the growth of an all-powerful, omni-present national government with all the perils of majority tyranny and soft despotism that was discussed above in chapter 4. Therefore, it is incumbent upon all the leadership in the Tea Party movement never to lose sight of this reality. Here are some pertinent reminders from Ben Stein:

> Don't let TV commentators get away with lies about our country. If you see someone telling a falsehood about America or about the way you know it to be, call them on it. Make sure they get mail setting them straight. ... If we make it clear that we don't like their attitude, we can sometimes get it changed. ... Support candidates you believe in. If you want men and women elected who believe in what you do, it's your job to get it done. Elections are lost because patriotic Americans assume that someone else will do it. That isn't so—it's not someone else's job; it's yours. So pass out literature, contribute what you can, make phone calls, ring doorbells, sign petitions, and so on. Get into the arena and work for what you believe in. And above all, vote. Brave men died to allow us to govern ourselves, so it's up to us to vindicate their belief and trust in the democratic system of a self-governing republic.[6]

Here is a reminder from Nicholas Wishek that is as pertinent today as it was four years ago. Back then he urged everyone to remember five to four when you go to vote. "Five to four. By one slim vote the court decided that I, as a law-abiding American citizen, should have the right to own a handgun to protect myself. I suspect our founding fathers would be shocked to see that they exchanged the tyranny of one man for the potential tyranny of nine. ... Five to four. If anyone doesn't realize how important the upcoming presidential election will be, some recent Supreme Court decisions should be an earsplitting warning of what would result from the [re-election] of Barack Obama."[7]

Be Willing to Pledge "Life, Fortune, and Sacred Honor"

In conformance with the rule of 150 that posits each of us have a limit as to how many people we can know and trust, it is vital that we work to encourage and persuade those with whom we maintain close relationships to get out and vote to replace the politicians currently adhering to the progressive/statist agenda. Dick Morris suggests the following action steps:

> Politics is no longer a spectator sport. Those in the grandstands must leave their seats and come down on the playing field to help their side score. … The days when the candidate and a small group of professionals ran things—and the rest of us chipped in money, showed up at rallies, and voted—are over. Now each of us must conduct our own campaign within our own circle of acquaintances, until the circle spreads to include thousands of voters. The Internet has made each of us the center of our own political campaign. We are the campaign. … In a way, political campaigns are coming full circle, to the way they were in the 19th century.… But in today's politics, those initiatives have to come from us, not from on high. … Political advertising, like all advertising, is losing its effectiveness —for two key reasons. First and most obviously, the Internet is replacing television.… But there is a second, more important reason that the conventional top-down media-driven political campaign isn't working anymore: because we don't believe what we hear from strangers. Our politicians suffer from a huge credibility gap. Advertisers face an even wider gap.… The more we disbelieve those we don't know, the more we do believe and rely upon those we do know. The old regimen of media propaganda is swiftly being supplanted by

old-fashioned word of mouth—recommendations from friends, trusted colleagues, and established, credible commentators—as our main source of information.[8]

For citizens willing to defend constitutional conservatism and do battle with the forces of the status quo represented by the Cognoscenti, it is important to remember that neither of the two major parties—Democrats and Republicans—can claim a majority within the electorate. The balance of power rests with those in the middle—the political independents and the ideological moderates—who tend to vote based upon the issues that are most important to them. These are the voters who must be contacted, challenged and made aware of the threat of an inevitable serfdom.

In my opinion, it is absolutely necessary for all Americans to take an active part in the electoral process. If we do not, we forfeit the results to those who were willing to put their bodies on the line. The signers of the Declaration of Independence pledged "their lives, fortunes and sacred honor." They were willing to risk their property and their lives to establish this new nation conceived in liberty. Can we do anything less to protect and preserve the freedom, opportunity and prosperity that we have enjoyed? Are we willing to step up and fight for what we believe? Now is the time to take a stand remembering that the Declaration of Independence is "the apple of gold" and the Constitution is the "frame of silver." That is the legacy we have enjoyed as our blessing. We can do no less for our children, grandchildren and their progeny.

Appendix :
Sources available to become a
more knowledgeable citizen

All the books listed in the bibliography, below, were very helpful in providing the context to really appreciate how serious is the problem represented by the ruling class—the Cognoscenti. For the general reader, Schweikart and Allen's *A Patriot History of the United States* provides a very readable resource. For those interested in learning more about the beginnings of the progressive/statist agenda, Pestritto and Atto's *American Progressivism* provides a very good overview. For those who would like to improve their understanding of the Declaration of Independence and the Federal Constitution, an excellent resource is the online "Constitution 101" course available through the Hillsdale College website that can be pursued at times convenient for you.

Civil War

An epic poem by Stephen Vincent Benet about the origins and tragedy of the Civil War, called "John Brown's Body," was once standard issue for American readers. James McPherson's *Battle Cry of Freedom* is an inspiring book. The entire series of Civil War books by Bruce Catton is a quick but detailed history of our greatest crisis.

World War II

Flags of Our Fathers by Bradley and Powers tells the story of the men who raised the Stars and Stripes over Mt. Suribachi on Iwo Jima in 1945. James Bradley also wrote *Flyboys*, about US flyers in World War II. *The Rise and Fall of the Third Reich* by William I. Shirer is a must-read. *Band of Brothers* by Stephen Ambrose is particularly good. *Victory at Sea*, a video collection from NBC, tells the naval side of the war. *Battlefield* is a series of videos of the great battles and campaigns of World War II that were fought all around the world.

Communism

The Russian Century by Brian Moynahan tells the story of what life and death in Russia were like, starting with the first stirrings of the most evil doctrine in history, communism. *The Black Book of Communism* by Stephane Courtis catalogues the casualty rate from communism, putting it between 85 and 100 million innocent souls. Reading this book will leave you aghast that so many Americans still defend communism as an ideologically noble endeavor. *Gulag* by Anne Applebaum is an account of how the vast prison system worked in the Soviet Union.

The series of nine books on Communism and anti-Communism by the great historians John Earl Haynes and Harvey Klehr illustrate how totally hoodwinked the intellectual class in America often was—even when they knew what was happening. These books can be located on Google by entering either author's name.

Other Resources

Eyes on the Prize is an inspiring documentary available on DVD and video. It shows how battles for the civil rights movement were fought in the 1950s and 1960s.

The Statistical Abstract of the United States is published by the Government Printing Office contains a wealth of background information.

What's So Great About America by Dinesh D'Souza lays out just how well America is doing by historic and geographic standards.

There are also some great newspapers that take consistently pro-American points of view and instill in readers a sense of the nation's greatness. The most vital daily read is *The Wall Street Journal*, especially the editorial page. *The Washington Times, The American Spectator, The National Review, The Weekly Standard*, and *The American Enterprise* are rich sources of sense and sensibility. Subscribe to all of them, discuss them within your family, and give them as gift subscriptions—they'll keep you centered around gratitude and patriotism.

The Heritage Foundation has an annual income of $30 million, employs around two hundred people, and holds some 700 lectures, debates and conferences a year. The Cato Institute preaches libertarianism. Former AEI fellows founded the Center for Strategic and International Studies. The Center for Security Policy focuses on foreign policy. The Ethics and Public Policy Center tries to bring "the Judeo-Christian moral tradition" to bear on political debate.

There are now about fifty conservative think tanks across the country, (compared with just a handful of liberal ones). These include The Hudson Institute in Wisconsin and The Hoover Institution in California (home for Milton Friedman, George Shultz and Gary Becker).

Become better informed on American history and government by reading David Barton, Prietto, et al. Be knowledgeable about tyranny from reading Huxley's *Brave New World,* Orwell's *1984* and *Animal Farm,* Tammy Bruce *The New Thought Police*, and Saul Alinsky's *Rules for Radicals.* Pay attention to the machinations of billionaire George Soros and the organizations he funds, i.e. ACORN.

Thomas Sowell has pondered the problem of two different political narratives at work in America. He condensed his thinking into the book *A Conflict of Visions: Ideological Origins of political struggles* (2007). He labels the two narratives as the "constrained" and "unconstrained" visions. The former puts attention on the realities of life and making arrangements that are predictable and well-known. The latter puts attention on the idealistic life and foregoes the predictable and well-known in favor of experimentation and improvisation.

For those interested in exploring the exemplary thinkers that fall within the camp of Sowell's constrained vision: Frederic Bastiat, Adam Smith, Thomas Hobbes, Edmund Burke, *The Federalist*, Thomas Malthus, Alexis de Tocqueville, Oliver Wendell Holmes, F.A. Hayek, William Buckley, and Milton Friedman.

For those interested in exploring the exemplary thinkers that fall within the camp of Sowell's unconstrained vision: William Godwin, Jean-Jacques Rousseau, Thomas Paine, Condorcet, Fourier, Harold Laski, Thorstein Veblen, John Kenneth Galbraith, and Ronald Dworkin.

Notes

In citing works in the notes, short titles have generally been used. Works frequently cited have been identified by the following abbreviations:

CRB   Citations taken from the Claremont Review of Books, published quarterly at Claremont, CA by the Claremont Institute.

OCR   Citations that are taken from the *Orange County Register*, Editorial page. The *Orange County Registe*r is a Freedom Communications newspaper.

Prog.   Ronald Pestritto and William J. Atto, eds. *American Progressivism: a reader.* Lanham, MD: Lexington Books, Rowman & Littlefield Publishers, Inc. 2008.

Preface

1- Free online dictionary

1. The apple of gold, the frame of silver and statism

1- Kevin Portteus, Lecture 8, Hillsdale College video course, "Constitution 101," 2012. http://constitution.hillsdale.edu/

2- John Locke, *Second Treatise of Government* (Indianapolis, IN: Hackett Publishing Company, Inc. 1980), xvi.

3- *Ibid.*, xx.

4- Joseph Melusky, *The Constitution: Our written legacy* (Malabar, Fl: Krieger Publishing Company, 1991), 23.

5- Rush Limbaugh, "The Americans who risked everything" reprinted from http://www.rushlimbaugh.com/home/daily/site 121500/content/extra.html.

6 - Glen Beck, Joshua Charles, Kevin Balfe and Wynton Hall. *The Original Argument. The Federalists' case for the Constitution, adapted for the 21ˢᵗ century.* (New York: Mercury Radio Arts/Threshold Editions, Inc., of Simon & Shuster, Inc. 20110, 13.

7 - *Ibid.*, 7.

8 – *Ibid.*, 47.

9 – *Ibid.*, 53.

10 – Hamilton, Madison and Jay, *The Federalist Papers* (New York, Mentor Books, 1961), 321.

11 – Beck, *Original Argument*, 145.

12 – *Ibid.*,151.

13 – *Ibid.*, 237.

14 – *Ibid.*, 272-273.

15 – *Ibid.*, 278.

16 – John Micklethwait and Adrian Wooldridge. *The Right Nation: conservative power in America.* (New York, the Penguin Press, 2004), 317.

17 - Henry V. Jaffa. "Lincoln in Peoria." CRB, F 2009, 55.

18 – G. W. F. Hegel. *Hegel's Philosophy of Right.* (Oxford University Press paperback, 1967), 132.

19 - Jonah Goldberg. *Liberal Fascism: The secret history of the American Left from Mussolini to the Politics of Meaning.* (New York: Doubleday Broadway Publishing Group, Random House, Inc. 2007), 95.

20 – Prog., 5.

21 - Prog., 4-6.

22 - Goldberg. *Liberal Fascism.* P. 86

23 - *Ibid.* p. 95

24 – Prog., 11.

2. The progressive movement and eroding the federal Constitution

1 - Prog., 2-3.

2 - Prog., 15-16.

3 - Prog., 18-19.

4 - Prog., 20-21.

5 – George Will. "The hubris of reason: Obama prefers a professor's approach to our complex problems." OCR, March 11, 2010.

6 - Prog., 3.

7 - Prog., 15.

8 - Charles R. Kesler and John B. Kienker, editors. *Life, Liberty and the Pursuit of Happiness: Ten years of the Claremont Review of Books.* (Lanham, MD: Rowman & Littlefield Publishers, Inc., 2012), 18.

9 - Prog., 17.

10 - Kesler. *Life, Liberty and the Pursuit of Happiness.* 31.

11 – *Ibid.* p. 35

12 - Prog. P. 26

13 – Kesler. *Life, Liberty and the Pursuit of Happiness.* P. 24

14 - Thomas Sowell. "Back to the future?" OCR March 28, 2012.

15 – Burton W. Folsom, *New Deal or Raw Deal? How FDR's economic legacy has damaged America.* (New York: Threshold Editions, Simon & Schuster, Inc. 2008), 258-59.

16 - Kesler. *Life, Liberty and the Pursuit of Happiness,* 13.

17 – Thomas Sowell. See note 14.

18 – Folsom. *New Deal of Raw Deal?,* 256 – 257.

19 – Micklethwait. *The Right Nation.* 66.

20 - Ben Stein and Phil DeMuth. *Can America Survive? The rage of the Left, the truth, and what to do about it.* (Carlsbad, CA: New Beginnings Press, Hay House, Inc. 2004), 60-61.

21 - Micklethwait. *The Right Nation,* 64.

22 - Goldberg. *Liberal Fascism,* 149.

23 - Earl Black and Merle Black. *Divided America: The ferocious power struggle in American politics.* (New York: Simon & Shuster, Inc. 2007), 38.

24 - Micklethwait. *The Right Nation,* 69.

25 - Goldberg. *Liberal Fascism,* 212-213

26 - Micklethwait. *The Right Nation,* 323.

27 – *Ibid.,* 116 – 119.

28 – *Ibid.,* 126-127.

29 – Milton Friedman and Rose Freidman. *Tyranny of the Status Quo.* (Orlando, Fl: Harcourt Brace Jovanovich, Publishers, 1983, 1984), 42.

30 – *Ibid.,* 45-46.

31 – Walter Williams. "Moral and immoral government" OCR, December 12, 2010.

32 – Steve Chapman. "Washington fever worse than flu." OCR, May 5, 2009.

33 – Kesler. *Life, Liberty and the Pursuit of Happiness.* P. 15

34 – Dick Morris and Eileen McGann. *2010 Take back America a battle plan: The stakes, the targets, the strategy and what you can do.* (New York: HarperCollins Publishers, 2010), 19-20.

35 – Williams. Refer to note 31.

36 – Friedman. *Tyranny of the Status Quo,* 43-45.

37 – George Will. "New Deal's roots run deep." OCR, July 12, 2007.

38 – Robert Samuelson. "Absurd farm subsidies." OCR, September 16, 2007.

39 – John Stossel. "Government largesse: stranger than fiction." OCR, August 21, 2006.

40 – Walter Williams. "Solutions creating more problems." OCR, May 14, 2008.

41 – Thomas Sowell. "Road to disaster paved with good intentions." OCR, May 10, 2009.

42 – Stein. *Can America Survive?* P. 66-67

43 – Walter Williams. "Seeing black racism for what it is." OCR, July 29, 2010.

44 – Tom Purcell. "A new Declaration of Independence." OCR, July 3, 2008.

3. The Cognoscenti: A New Aristocracy and Academic Indoctrination

1 – Robert H. Bork. *Slouching to Gomorrah: Modern liberalism and American decline.* (New York: Regan Books, Harper Collins Publishers, 1996.), 7.

2 – Thomas Sowell. "To do big damage, it takes high IQs." OCR, September 30, 2009.

3 - Goldberg. *Liberal Fascism,* 158-9.

4 - Stein. *Can America Survive?,* 159-163.

5 – Malcolm Gladwell. *The Tipping Point: How little things can make a big difference.* (New York: Little, Brown and Company, 2000, 2002), 179-183.

6 – Lexington. "Minding about the gap." *The Economist,* June 11, 2005.

7 – Jerome Kabel. "Merit in motion." *The Economist,* November 26, 2005.

8 – Editorial. "The ruling class: the gap between what federal workers and private-sector workers make is growing wider." OCR, June 7, 2006.

9 - Morris. *2010 Take back America a battle plan,* 30-31.

10 - Editorial. "Civil servants paid more like masters. US government staffers make, on average, double that of typical private-sector staff." OCR, August 8, 2010.

11 – Gary Jason. "Obama's surge in government jobs. Federal workforce, compensation have grown during recession." OCR, February 23, 2010.

12 - Brian Calle. "City manager's $800k salary exposes a ruling class." OCR, July 13, 2011.

13 – Associated press. "Governor gives staff plum jobs." OCR, November 22, 2006.

14 – Daniel Weintraub. "A case study in looting: Engineers' outrageous contract one more painful legacy of the Davis era." OCR, March 19, 2004.

15 – Ian Murray. *Stealing you Blind: How government fat cats are getting rich off of you.* (Washington D. C. Regnery Publishing, Inc. 2011), 177.

16 - Bork. *Slouching to Gomorrah,* 4.

17 – *Ibid.,* 84.

18 – Daniel J. Flynn. *Intellectual Morons: How ideology makes smart people fall for stupid Ideas.* (New York: Three Rivers press, Crown Publishing Group, Random House, Inc. 2004), 1-3

19 – *Ibid.,* 4-8.

20 – *Ibid.,* 14-15.

21 - Stein. *Can America Survive?,* 138 –139.

22 – *Ibid.,* xxviii.

23 – George F. Will. "Campus commissars: Only one ideology is tolerated among today's faculty. So much for diversity." OCR, November 26, 2004.

24 – Thomas Potase. "Liberal bias on campus? Been there, done that." OCR, December 4, 2004.

25 – Herb Meyers. "Political Prisms." Speech given to Women of Washington in Seattle, July 31, 2008. Accessed from American Thinker, February 27, 2012. http://www.american thinker.com/2008/07/political_prisms.html

26 - Kesler. *Life, Liberty and the Pursuit of Happiness,* 3.

27 – Walter Williams. "Who to blame for college's sorry state." OCR, August 2, 2006.

28 – George F. Will. *"Conservatives need not apply." OCR, October 16, 2007.*

29 - Stein. *Can America Survive?,* xxix – xxx.

30 – *Ibid.,* 150-54.

31 – John Tierney. "You wanna talk cronies? A liberal monoculture prevails in institutions of law and journalism." OCR, October 12, 2005.

32 – Thomas Sowell. "Lawmaking run amok. More and more, the Constitution is a nuisance to judges, politicians." OCR, December 29, 2010.

33 - Robert H. Bork. *The Tempting of America: The political seduction of the law.* (New York: A Touchstone Book, Simon & Schuster, 1991), 3.

34 – *Ibid.,* 9.

35– Morton Kondracke. "Democrats will set the tone. Hopes for a 'dignified process' for confirming Supreme Court justices rest with the party that invented 'Borking' and the judicial filibuster." OCR, July 14, 2005.

4. Tipping into majority tyranny and soft despotism

1 – Jared Diamond. *Guns, Germs and Steel: The fates of human societies.* (New York: W. W. Norton & Company, 1997,1999), 124-5.

2 – *Ibid.,* 272.

3 – *Ibid.,* 274-275.

4 – Adams, John. *A Defence of the Constitutions of Government of the United States of America, 1787* Letter III hua.umf.maine.edu/Reading_Revolutions/Adams.html.

5 – Walter Williams. "Future prospects for economic Liberty. Lecture delivered August 2, 2009 on a Hillsdale College cruise aboard the Crystal Sernity. IMPRIMIS, vol. 38, no. 9, September, 2009.

6 – Alexis de Tocqueville. *Democracy in America (*New York: Barnes & Noble Books, 2003), 229

7 – *Ibid,* 235.

8 - *Ibid.,* 236.

9 - Mark R. Levin. *Ameritopia: The unmaking of America.* (New York: Simon & Shuster, Inc., 2012), xi.

10 – Mark Steyn. "Wait and see how flexible he'll be." OCR, April 8, 2012.

11 - Stein. *Can America Survive?,* 173-175.

12 – John Micklethwait and Adrian Wooldridge. *The Right Nation: conservative power in America.* (New York, the Penguin Press, 2004), 322.

13 - *Ibid.,* 67.

14 – Jonah Goldberg. *Liberal Fascism.* (New York: Doubleday Broadway PublishingGroup, Random House, Inc. 2007), 180.

15 – Robert H. Bork. *Slouching to Gomorrah: Modern liberalism and American decline* (New York: Regan Books, Harper Collins Publishers, 1996), 26-27.

16 – *Ibid.,* 55.

17 – *Ibid.,* 54.

18 – David Horowitz. "To Have And Have Not: Alinsky, Beck, Satan and Me, Part IV." Front Page Magazine. August 19, 2009, http://archive.frontpagemag.com/readBlog.aspx?BLOGID=1051

19 – Stephen Ohlemacher, AP. "Minorities a majority in 10% of counties: Cultural conflicts arise in some areas as demographic patterns change." OCR, August 9, 2007.

20 – David Dickey. "Few say 'no, thanks' to government. With it controlling so many resources, resistance can seem futile." OCR, November 30, 2010.

21 – Burton W. Folsom Jr.. *New Deal or Raw Deal? How FDR's economic legacy has damaged America.* (New York: Simon & Schuster, Inc. 2008), 255.

22 – Goldberg. *Liberal Fascism,* 89.

23 – Ronald Pestritto and William J. Atto, eds. *American Progressivism.* (Lanham, MD: Lexington Books, Rowman & Littlefield Publishers, Inc. 2008), 26.

24 – Angelo M. Codevilla. "The chosen one: the rise and rise of Obama." *Claremont Review of Books*, Volume XI, Number 3, Summer 2011.

25 – Dick Morris. *2010 Take back America a battle plan:* (New York: HarperCollins Publishers, 2010), 9.

26 – *Ibid.,* 17-18.

5. Become a knowledgeable citizen.

1 – Alan W. Bock. "Our enemy, the State." OCR, July 30, 2006.

2 - Ian Murray. *Stealing you Blind:* (Washington D. C.: Regnery Publishing, Inc. 2011), 9.

3 – *Ibid.,* 11.

4 – Rich Lowry. "Obama punctures cultural nerve. Discontent isn't just about fiscal probity but American way of life." OCR, March 1, 2010.

5 – Victor Davis Hanson. "Flexible moral outrage. Progressives enraged at the 'sins' of others, forgiving of their own." OCR, June 2, 2011.

6 – Thomas Sowell. "You've made enough…What some people call social justice is really anti-social politics." OCR, May 19, 2010.

7 – Walter Williams. "Americans today, founders at odds." OCR, July 7, 2010.

8 - Steve Chapman. "Daley's not done on handguns. He wants training, registration and a limit of one per person." OCR, July 5, 2010.

9 – *District of Columbia* v. *Heller*, (No.07-290) Justice Stevens dissenting. http://www.law.cornell.edu/supct/html/07-290.ZD.html

10 – John Tierney. "Laura Bush vs. red-state stereotypes." OCR, May 4, 2005.

11 – David Brooks. "Tribalism still trumps integration. The dream of all of us living together may not fit with how we really are." OCR, July 11, 2007.

12 – Lolita Baldour, AP. "Pentagon, governors in face-off on reserves. A fight concerns natural disasters." OCR, August 14, 2009. .

13 – Gene Healy and Benjamin Friedman, CATO Institute. "Be wary of using military as police." OCR, December 26, 2008.

14 – Paul Wishek. "The founders wanted us to be well-armed. Unlike today's government, they treated citizens as adults." OCR, August 8, 2008.

6. Reform government spending and reduce Federal deficits

1 –Walter Williams. "America's deficit of political guts." OCR, August 12, 2010.

2 – Robert J. Samuelson. "'Easy road' heading for dead end. Neither party tackles tough problems until there's a calamity." OCR, September 2, 2009.

3. – Walter Williams. "What about upholding the Constitution?" OCR, April 9, 2008.

4 – Morton Kondracke. "Our kids will pay for our profligacy." OCR, February 1, 2005.

5 – Robert J. Samuelson. "Rise up, young voters. You're getting shafted to pay for old peoples' retirements." OCR, October 23, 2008.

6 – Walter Williams. "Cost of saving the nation." OCR, January 30, 2011.

7 - David Brooks, "Flailing and failing." OCR, June 3, 2003

8 - Murray, Ian. *Stealing you Blind:* (Washington D. C.: Regnery Publishing, Inc. 2011), 91.

9 - Murray. *Stealing you Blind.* p. 174 -185

10 – *Ibid.* p. 177

11 – *Ibid.* p. 183-184

12 – *Ibid.* p. 177-178

13 – *Ibid.* p. 179

14 - *Ibid.* p. 184-185

15 – *Ibid.* p. 177

16 – *Ibid.* p. 48

17 – *Ibid.* p. 45

18 – *Ibid.* p. 48

7. Reform the Federal tax code and increase revenues

1 - David Dickey. "Few say 'no, thanks' to government." OCR, November 30, 2010.

2 - Walter Williams. "Tax evil rich? Let's do the math." OCR, April 12, 2011

3 - Thomas Sowell. "GOP needs bigger punch. Facts favor Republicans, but liberals jab with repetitious rhetoric." OCR, February 16, 2011.

4 - George F. Will. *Suddenly.* (New York: Free Press, Macmillan Inc.), 168

5 - Friedman. *Tyranny of the Status Quo*, 63 –67.

6 - Murray. *Stealing you Blind.* p. 179 –181.

8. Reclaim control over public education

1 – Murray. *Stealing you Blind*, 89 –90.

2. – Larry Schweikart and Michael Allen. *A Patriot's History of the United States.* (New York: Sentinel, the Penguin Group, 2007), xiii.

3 – Gary Jason. "Spending more for less. Administrative bloat hurting US higher education." OCR, September 12, 2010.

4 - Murray. *Stealing you Blind*, 186.

5 – Dan Walters. "No link between money, graduates." OCR, May 10, 2006.

6 – Dan Walters. "Stats refute school spending rhetoric." OCR, April 3, 2008.

7 - George F. Will. "A system slow to learn. Lots of union teachers, faddish social experiments, NCLB haven't helped schools." OCR, April 24, 2008.

8 – Bill Evers and Ze'ev Wurman. "Reader rebuttal: algebra in eighth grade." OCR, March 13, 2011.

9 – Thomas Sowell. "The illusion of education reform." *The Modesto Bee*, December 10, 1999.

10 – George F. Will. "Helping U.S. students catch up to the world." OCR, January 30, 2011.

11 – Walter Williams. "Monopoly makes America stupid." OCR, June 12, 2007.

12 - Stein Ben and Phil DeMuth. *Can America Survive?* (Carlsbad, CA: New Beginnings Press, Hay House Inc. 2004), 197.

13 – John Stossel. School choice a new world. Freedom and competition will produce creative new options." OCR, March 6, 2006.

14 - Vicki Murray. "School reform not about resources." OCR, May 15, 2007.

15 - Vicki Murray. "Voucher movement wins another round." OCR, June 20, 2007.

16 - John Stossel. "Government money taints its recipients." OCR, November 8,

2007.

17 – Star Parker. "The monopoly's got to end." OCR, April 10, 2005.

18 – Alan Bonsteel. "Spending more, getting less. Per-pupil spending in public schools sets new high, as does dropout rate." OCR, August 29, 2007.

19 - Murray. *Stealing you Blind,* 185.

20 – Ari J. Kaufman. "Heels dug in against 'change.' The word is being widely used, but don't speak it about public education." OCR, January 27, 2008.

21 –John Leo. "Choice words for teacher unions." *U.S. News & World Report,* March 11, 1996.

22 – John Stossel. "Teachers unions vent, but can't refute." OCR, March 10, 2007.

Fight to avoid an inevitable serfdom

1 – Friedrich von Hayek, *The Road to Serfdom.* University of Chicago Press, 16th impression 1962, xiv.

2 – Dick Morris. *2010 Take back America a battle plan:* (New York: HarperCollins Publishers, 2010), 30-31.

3 – William Voegeli. "The meaning of the Tea Party." *Claremont Review of Books*, Volume X, Number 3, Summer 2010.

4 - *Ibid.* Summer 2010.

5 – Nicholas Wishek. "Liberals' dream, America's nightmare. Country can't afford utopian goal of cradle-to-grave support." OCR, August 17, 2011.

6 - Stein. *Can America Survive?,* 197-198.

7 – Nicholas Wishek. "Remember '5-4' when you go to vote!" OCR, July 22, 2008.

8 – Morris. *2010 Take back, 295*

Bibliography

Adams, John. *A Defence of the Constitutions of Government of the United States of America, 1787* hua.umf.maine.edu/Reading_Revolutions/**Adams**.html

Beck, Glenn and Joshua Charles, Kevin Balfe and Wynton Hall. *The Original Argument. The Federalists' case for the Constitution, adapted for the 21*[st] *century.* New York: Mercury Radio Arts/Threshold Editions, Inc., of Simon & Shuster, Inc. 2011

Beck, Glenn with Joseph Kerry. *Glenn Beck's Common Sense*: *The case against an out-of-control government, inspired by Thomas Paine.* New York: Mercury Radio Arts/Threshold Editions, Inc., of Simon & Shuster, Inc. 2009

Black, Earl and Merle Black. *Divided America: The ferocious power struggle in American politics.* New York: Simon & Shuster, Inc. 2007

Bork, Robert H. *Slouching to Gomorrah: Modern liberalism and American decline.* New York: ReganBooks, an imprint of HarperCollinsPublishers, 1996

____ *The Tempting of America: The political seduction of the law.* New York: A Touchstone Book, Simon & Shuster, 1991

Burke, Edmund. *The Portable Edmund Burke*. ed. with an introduction by IsaacKraminick. New York: Penguin Putnam, Inc. 1999

Curtis, Michael, ed. *The Great Political Theories, Vol. 2: from Burke, Rousseau and Kant to modern times*. New York: Avon Books, an imprint of HarperCollins publishers, 1962, 1981

Diamond, Jared. *Guns, Germs and Steel: The fates of human societies*. New York: W. W. Norton & Company, 1997, 1999

Flynn, Daniel J. *Intellectual Morons: How ideology makes smart people fall for stupid Ideas*. New York: Three Rivers press, imprint of Crown Publishing Group, Random House, Inc. 2004

Folsom, Burton W. Jr.. *New Deal or Raw Deal? How FDR's economic legacy has damaged America*. New York: Threshold Editions, Simon & Schuster, Inc. 2008

Friedman, Milton & Rose Freidman. *Tyranny of the Status Quo*. Orlando, Fl: Harcourt Brace Jovanovich, Publishers, 1983, 1984

Gladwell, Malcolm. *The Tipping Point: How little things can make a big difference*. New York: Little, Brown and Company, 2000, 2002

Goldberg, Jonah. *Liberal Fascism: The secret history of the American Left from Mussolini to the Politics of Meaning*. New York: Doubleday Broadway Publishing Group, Random House, Inc. 2007

Greenberg, Stanley B. *The Two Americas: Our current political deadlock and how to break it*. New York: Thomas Dunne books, St. Martin's Press, 2004

Hamilton, Alexander, James Madison and John Jay. *The Federalist Papers*. Introduction by Clinton Rossiter. New York: Mentor Books, the New American Library of World Literature, Inc., 1961

Hayek, Freidrich von. *The Road to Serfdom.* University of Chicago Press, Chicago 37 Rutledge and Kegan Paul London Univ. of Toronto Press 1944. 16ᵗʰ impression 1962

Hegel, G.W. F. *Hegel's Philosophy of Right.* Translated with notes by T. M. Knox. London: first published by the Clarendon Press, 952. First issued as an Oxford University Press paperback, 1967.

Himmelfarb, Gertrude. *One Nation, Two Cultures: A searching examination of American society in the aftermath of our cultural revolution.* New York: Alfred A. Knopf, 1999.

Horowitz, David. *Left Illusions: an intellectual Odyssey.* ed. with an introduction by Jamie Glazov. Dallas: Spence Publishing Co., 2003.

Kesler, Charles R. and John B. Kienker, eds. *Life, Liberty and the Pursuit of Happiness: Ten years of the Claremont Review of Books.* Lanham, MD: Rowman & Littlefield Publishers, Inc. subsidiary of the Rowman & Littlefield Publishing Group, Inc., 2012

Kirk, Russell. *The Conservative Mind: from Burke to Eliot.* Seventh revised edition . Washington D. C.: Regnery Publishing, Inc. 1953, 1995.

Koch, Adrienne, ed. *The American Enlightenment: the shaping of the American experiment and a free society.* New York: George Braziller, Inc. 1965

Levin, Mark R. *Ameritopia: The unmaking of America.* New York: Threshold Editions, a division of Simon & Shuster, Inc., 2012

Locke, John. *Second Treatise of Government.* ed. by C. B. Macpherson. Originally published in 1690. Indianapolis, IN: Hackett Publishing Company, Inc. 1980

Melusky, Joseph. *The Constitution: Our written legacy.* Malabar, Fl: Krieger Publishing Company, 1991.

Micklethwait, John and Adrian Wooldridge. *The Right Nation: conservative power in America.* New York, the Penguin Press, 2004.

Morris, Dick and Eileen McGann. *2010 Take back America a battle plan: The stakes, the targets, the strategy … and what you can do.* New York: HarperCollins Publishers, 2010.

Murray, Ian. *Stealing you Blind: How government fat cats are getting rich off of you.* Washington D. C.: Regnery Publishing, Inc. 2011.

Pestritto, Ronald and William J. Atto, eds. *American Progressivism: a reader.* Lanham, MD: Lexington Books, Rowman & Littlefield Publishers, Inc. 2008.

Schweikart, Larry and Michael Allen. *A Patriot's History of the United States: from Columbus's great discovery to the war on terror.* New York: Sentinel, published by the Penguin Group, 2007.

Shlaes, Amity. *The Forgotten Man: a new history of the Great Depression.* New York: Harper Collins Publishers, Harper Perennial edition, 2008

Sowell, Thomas. *A Conflict of Visions: ideological origins of political struggles.* New York: Basic Books, Penguin Books Group, 2007

Stein Ben and Phil DeMuth. *Can America Survive? The rage of the Left, the truth, and what to do about it.* Carlsbad, CA: New Beginnings Press, an imprint of Hay House, Inc. 2004.

Tocqueville, Alexis de. *Democracy in America.* Originally published vol. I, 1835, vol. II, 1840. First published in this format by Ticknor and Fields, 1862. Translated by Henry Reeve, Esq. Edited, with Notes by Francis

Bowen. Introduction by Eric W. Plaag. New York: Barnes & Noble Books, 2003.

Watson, Peter. *The Modern Mind: an intellectual history of the 20*[th] *century*. Originally published in Great Britain by Weidenfield & Nicolson, 2000. New York: Harper Collins, Perennial edition, 2002

Will, George F. *Suddenly: The American idea abroad and at home 1986-1990*. New York: The Free press, a division of Macmillan, Inc., 1990

www.ingramcontent.com/pod-product-compliance
Lightning Source LLC
Chambersburg PA
CBHW071357310526
45789CB00020B/463